HEALTH & WEALTH:
How Social and Economic Factors Affect Our Well-Being

By Monica Townson

published by
The Canadian Centre for Policy Alternatives
and distributed by
James Lorimer and Co. Ltd.
1999

Canadian Cataloguing in Publication Data

Townson, Monica, 1932-
Health and wealth: how social and economic factors affect
our well being

Includes index.
ISBN 1-55028-659-5 (bound) ISBN 1-55028-658-7 (pbk.)

1. Health status indicators – Canada. 2. Social status –
Health aspects – Canada. 3. Canada – Social policy. I. Title.

RA407.5.C3T68 1999   362.1'042'0971   C99-930336-8

Printed and bound in Canada

Published by
The Canadian Centre for Policy Alternatives
804-251 Laurier Avenue West
Ottawa, Ontario, K1P 5J6

Distributed by
James Lorimer & Company Ltd., Publishers
35 Britain Street
Toronto, Ontario M5A 1R7

TABLE OF CONTENTS

Chapter 1   1
The Health of the Population

Chapter 2   21
Inequalities in Health

ACKNOWLEDGMENTS

We wish to acknowledge the Population Health Fund of Health Canada for its financial contribution to this study and John Horvath and the Adult Health Division of Health Canada for their initiative and support.

EXECUTIVE SUMMARY

For the past 25 years, Canada has been pursuing an agenda to promote the health of the Canadian population and is officially committed to the goal set by the World Health Organization of "Health for All by the Year 2000." In recent years, the policy emphasis seems to have shifted from one of "health promotion," which encouraged people to increase control over and improve their own health, to focus more on "population health" — described as an approach that addresses the entire range of factors that determine health and, by so doing, affects the health of the entire population.

There appears to be considerable confusion between the two approaches, but both acknowledge that socioeconomic factors are key influences in the health of populations. Federal, Provincial and Territorial Ministers of Health, who meet regularly to consider strategies to improve the health of the Canadian population, have also acknowledged that living and working conditions, early childhood development and physical environment are major influences on population health.

Reports prepared for the deputy ministers of health have outlined in some detail strategies to address some of these socioeconomic factors and to develop a more integrated approach to health. Health officials have acknowledged the key things that need to be done, such as creating a thriving and sustainable economy with meaningful work for all; ensuring an adequate income for all Canadians; reducing the number of families living in poverty; ensuring an equitable distribution of income; and making sure there is suitable, adequate and affordable housing.

There is now a very extensive world-wide literature on health inequalities and the socioeconomic factors that are responsible for them. Researchers have long documented the impact on health of poverty and unemployment, poor housing and lack of education, child poverty and problems in early childhood development. They have also noted how all these elements are inter-connected. Unemployment may bring poverty; poverty may determine the type of housing a family has; lack of education may limit earning power; poverty and early childhood development may limit the educational opportunities people have.

All of these influences may explain why some people are healthy and others are not. But they do not explain why the population of some countries appears to be healthier than the population of others. If health inequalities were due to poverty, for instance, why have they increased in countries such as Britain during the last fifty years, despite huge rises in the standard of living? Why is life expectancy higher in countries like Greece, Japan, Iceland and Italy than it is in richer countries like the United States or Germany?

Researchers are now finding that, in the developed world, it is not the richest countries which have the best health, but the most egalitarian. According to British author Richard Wilkinson, in a recent book, *Unhealthy Societies: the Afflictions of Inequality,* the quality of the social life of a society is one of the most powerful determinants of health. And this, in turn, is very closely related to the degree of income inequality.

Public policies that contribute to increasing income inequality are also likely to result in deteriorating population health. The case of Britain under the Conservative government of Margaret Thatcher provides startling evidence of this. As Thatcherite policies of radical marketization took hold, around 1978-1979, inequality in incomes began to rise. The lowest income groups did not benefit from economic growth; the proportion of the population with less than half the average income more than trebled; the gap between low wages and high wages grew; and polarization between deprived neighbourhoods and affluent neighbourhoods gradually increased.

By the late 1980s in Britain, the effects of widening income differences on local disparities and on the rate of reduction in national mortality rates were already evident. As deprivation in some areas increased, mortality rates in some age groups in the poorest areas actually rose. In other age groups they simply failed to fall. Wilkinson says it's likely that similar processes affected mortality in the United States. As income differences widened there during the 1980s, the rate at which the population's life expectancy improved also slowed down. The national slow-down was associated particularly with a decline in life expectancy among the black population.

In Canada, the health of First Nations people is a shocking example of the impact of socioeconomic conditions on health. Government reports acknowledge that Canada's Aboriginal people, as a group, are the most disadvantaged of all citizens, and have the poorest overall health status. Their life expectancy is still seven years less than that of the overall Canadian population and there are almost twice as many infant deaths among Aboriginal peoples — a higher rate than the poorest neighbourhoods of Canada.

According to the Canadian Public Health Association, poor social conditions, such as lack of jobs and access to a clean water supply, physical and social isolation, substandard and crowded housing, and a loss of cultural identity, all contribute to the poor health of First Nations people.

It is evident that Canada has not yet adopted strategies for improving population health by addressing socioeconomic conditions. For example, about 1.5 million children, or 21% of all Canada's children, now live in low-income families. That is 47% more than in 1989. About 61% of lone-parent families headed by women live below the poverty line, as do 53% of elderly women who are on their own.

Unemployment is still extremely high, even when measured by the official unemployment rate. And it has been estimated that only about 36% of those who are unemployed now qualify for unemployment benefits. Public commitment to social housing has been abandoned, and the number of people who are homeless is rising.

Perhaps most disturbing of all, the gap between rich and poor is widening. Statistics Canada reports that, because of economic downturns, the income gap between high- and low-income families grew significantly after 1980. The gap was reduced during the recovery of the 1980s. But the improvement was not enough to counter the inequality increases associated with the 1981-82 recession.

Taxes and government transfers during this time were able to bridge the gap between rich and poor, so that after-tax inequality did not increase. But in 1996, for the first time, after-tax inequality increased, too. StatsCan says lower-income families have not benefited form the latest advances in earnings to the same degree they did during the recovery of the late 1980s. Cutbacks in government transfer payments as a result of "program restructuring" meant that taxes and transfers were no longer able to offset the increases in pre-tax inequality.

Although politicians have officially made commitments to develop strategies for improving population health, they have not, to date, taken steps to address these socioeconomic developments. The National Forum on Health, which began a "Dialogue with Canadians" in the fall of 1995 by visiting 34 communities across Canada and holding discussion groups, released a consultation document in November 1996, based on two years of research and consultation. In a telling comment, the document says that, "Despite what is known about the determinants of health, the general public continues to be mainly concerned about health care, especially when services are perceived to be threatened. As well, *governments and public administrators have not demonstrated in their decisions any appreciation of the impact of social and economic determinants and their impact on the health of individuals and communities*"" (emphasis added).

Canadian authors Michael Hayes and James Dunn, in a recent study for the Canadian Policy Research Networks, observe that the policy implications stemming from the conclusion that by reducing material inequities within society we will improve overall health status and reduce inequities in health, would require the body politic to overcome the entrenched asymmetries of power. Ruling élites are not easily persuaded to relinquish power, these authors point out, and the economic and cultural structures that maintain inequities nationally and internationally are not easily transformed.

Change, however, is by no means impossible. As anthropologist Margaret Mead has wisely reminded us, "Never doubt that a small group of thoughtful, committed citizens can change the world. Indeed, it's the only thing that ever has."

Chapter 1
THE HEALTH OF THE POPULATION

There is no doubt that the health of the population has become a major preoccupation of policy-makers, not only in Canada, but on a world-wide scale. As long ago as 1977, the World Health Assembly decided that the main social goal of governments and the World Health Organization in the last few decades of the 20th century should be "the attainment by all people of the world by the year 2000 of a level of health that would permit them to lead a socially and economically productive life."[1] National governments were scheduled to report in 1997 on their progress toward this goal, and global findings were to be reported to the WHO in 1998. Like most other goals set for the new millennium, it seems unlikely this one will be achieved.

However, during the 1970s, Canada was already pursuing an agenda to promote the health of the Canadian population. The basis for the government's approach was outlined in a 1974 federal publication, *A New Perspective on the Health of Canadians* — sometimes referred to as the Lalonde Report as it was issued by Marc Lalonde who was the Minister of Health at that time.[2] It put forward the view that people's health was influenced by a broad range of factors, including "human biology, lifestyle, the organization of health care, and the social and physical environments in which people live." While the statement acknowledges that social environment can affect health, the emphasis was very much on the "choices" individuals make to engage in unhealthy behaviour. According to the Report, "Personal decisions and habits that are bad from a health point of view create self-imposed risks. When those risks result in illness or death, the victim's lifestyle can be said to have contributed to, or caused, his own illness or death."[3] There was no acknowledgment that social and economic circumstances determine the kind of "choices" individuals can make.

Meeting the challenge of the World Health Organization

When the WHO issued its challenge to governments to outline plans for meeting its goal of "Health for All by the Year 2000," Canada's response was outlined in a 1986 publication called *Achieving Health for All: A Framework for Health Promotion.*[4] Although the approach was referred to as "health promotion," the government claimed it represented an expansion of the traditional use of that term. "We regard health promotion as an approach that complements and strengthens the existing system of health care," the government said.

According to this "new vision of health," as the government described it, the representation of the factors contributing to health legitimizes the idea of developing health policies and practices within a broader context. As evidence of its endorsement of the WHO definition of health promotion as "the process of enabling people to increase control over and to improve their health," the government pointed to initiatives it had taken to encourage moderation in drinking; to promote breast feeding; to discourage smoking; and to assist voluntary groups committed to undertaking health promotion activities.

It presented six strategies which it said would enable Canada to attain its aim of achieving health for all:

1. ensuring access to health information;
2. encouraging consensus about particular health ideas;
3. initiating research in support of health promotion;
4. fostering public participation;
5. advocating a strong role for the health care system, particularly for community health services; and
6. coordinating policies between sectors.

The government said that "The experience of the past ten years has confirmed our view that health promotion provides an avenue for dealing with emerging challenges, an approach which supports Canadians in improving the quality of their health. In summary, it offers a means of achieving health for all Canadians."[5]

But, while the government's report admitted that "The first challenge we face is to find ways of reducing inequities in the health of low- versus high-income groups in Canada," it offered no ideas on how that might be achieved. Implicit in its list of strategies is the emphasis on "health policies" — apparently implying the kind of policies departments of health had traditionally followed — and an approach that continued to emphasize the role of individuals in trying to improve their health by adopting healthy lifestyles.

Another of the leading challenges, said the government, was "that of enhancing people's capacity to cope." Healthy public policies, it said, "help to set the stage for health promotion, because they make it easier for people to make healthy choices." But the government admitted that "We cannot invite people to assume responsibility for their health and then turn around and fault them for illnesses and disabilities which are the outcome of wider social and economic circumstances. Such a 'blaming the victim' attitude is based on the unrealistic notion that the individual has ultimate and complete control over life and death."

Canada hosted the First International Conference on Health Promotion in Ottawa in 1986, where the *Ottawa Charter on Health Promotion* was adopted by the participating countries. It called for action to be taken to:

- **build healthy public policy** to ensure that policy developed by all sectors contributes to health-promoting conditions;
- **create supportive environments** (physical, social, economic, cultural, spiritual) that recognize the rapidly changing nature of society, particularly in the areas of technology and the organization of work, and that ensure positive impacts on the health of the people;
- **strengthen community action** so that communities have the capacity to set priorities and make decisions on issues that affect their health;
- **develop personal skills** to enable people to have the knowledge and skills to meet life's challenges and to contribute to society; and
- **reorient health services** to create systems which focus on the needs of the whole person and invite a true partnership among the providers and users of the services.[6]

But implementing these calls to action has apparently not been easy. According to some observers, there are a number of reasons for this. But perhaps one of the most important has been "the need to show how action directed at the underlying prerequisites or determinants can affect health."[7]

Health promotion and population health

It is important to emphasize that the terms "health promotion" and "population health" have particular and different meanings to those involved in the debate over health policy. To the uninitiated, the terms are confusing, to say the least.

According to one definition, "Health promotion is commonly defined as a process for enabling people to take control over and improve their health. Population health is an approach that addresses the entire range of factors that determine health and, by so doing, affects the health of the entire population.[8]

Although the two approaches evolved at roughly the same time, over the course of the 1990s, according to Michael Hayes and James Dunn, "population health has eclipsed health promotion in the rhetoric of contemporary health policy."

In a 1998 paper for the Canadian Policy Research Networks,[9] these authors explain that the development of **health promotion** was nurtured by the WHO throughout the early 1980s. It was a much more holistic concept of health than the prevailing biomedical model and, thanks to the efforts of a number of key players in Canada who wanted to expand the Lalonde model of health, "health promotion met with incredible success as a policy thrust and (bureaucratically driven) social movement."

From the beginning, say Hayes and Dunn, health promotion rhetoric and practice has emphasized community involvement and public participation — but it was mostly stimulated by bureaucratic funding and it tended to focus on an individual-centred response to health issues. Programs to discourage smoking, to emphasize *Participaction,* and to highlight the dangers of drinking and driving, were the kind of programs the government sponsored as part of its health promotion agenda — although many people outside the bureaucracy participated in health promotion activities. However, as these authors point out, "These types of responses were also very helpful to public servants pressured by the political sphere to 'do something' about the rising costs of health care services and growing awareness of social inequalities in health status, without wading too deeply into the ideological waters of social structure."[10]

Other critics say the health promotion approach individualizes both the root of the problem and many of the remedies. In this way, proponents of the approach were able to avoid challenging "either the conventional world of work, income distribution, and control over the environment, or the conventional medical establishment. It was politically much safer to exhort individuals to live better, often implicitly blaming them for their own illnesses."[11]

The **population health** approach, spearheaded in Canada by Dr. Fraser Mustard and the Canadian Institute for Advanced Research (CIAR), focuses on the interrelated conditions and factors that influence the health of populations. And, according to Dr. Mustard, who apparently coined the phrase "population health" to describe his approach, "Further enhancement of information in this area will give society an increased choice of whether it wishes to develop strategies to intervene with social and economic problems from the standpoint of prevention to modify the impact of cultural, economic and social factors on the health of populations, or whether we would prefer to increase the services of human care for individuals whose health becomes abnormal as a consequences of their genetic makeup and the environment in which they live."[12] In other words, society must choose if it wishes to address the fundamental causes of health inequalities, or if it will simply treat those whose health suffers as a result of those socioeconomic inequalities.

Population health, defined as "the label used to describe the analysis of major social, physical, behavioural and biological influences upon overall levels of health status within and between identifiable population groups and subgroups,"[13] has now come to dominate the debate on health policy in Canada — although, as a recent survey conducted for the Canadian Policy Research Networks Inc. found, "population health has barely begun to be understood, even among its advocates."[14] But Hayes and Dunn warn that it would be misleading to simply conclude that population health is concerned with the social determinants of health and that health promotion is concerned only with individual elements, even though much of what was done by governments and others in the name of health promotion did focus on changing individual behaviours.

The socioeconomic determinants of population health

Both health promotion and population health acknowledge that socioeconomic factors are key influences in the health of populations. Evidence of the socioeconomic determinants of health has been around for more than 100 years, in fact. In mid-nineteenth century Britain, for example, there were numerous studies of public health that measured death rates from different diseases in different locations and pinpointed the high incidence of disease in poor areas.[15] Such inequalities in health eventually led to the establishment of the British National Health Service in the 1940s.

However, a Research Working Group, appointed by the Secretary of State for Social Services of the Labour government in 1977 to investigate (among other things) why mortality rates of the poor had failed to improve since the health service was established, concluded that much of the problem lay outside the NHS. The Working Group on Inequalities in Health, which was chaired by Sir Douglas Black, then President of the Royal College of Physicians, reported in 1980. It found that "social and economic factors like income, work (or lack of it), environment, education, housing, transport, and what are today called 'lifestyles' all affect health and all favour the better-off. Yet they largely remained outside the ambit of national health policy."[16]

Recent research on the socioeconomic determinants of the health of populations has generated a very extensive literature analyzing virtually all countries of the world, including both industrialized and less developed countries. It is well known, for example, that poverty and unemployment result in poor health. And more recent work demonstrates clearly that income distribution is an even more important determinant of the health of populations.

In Canada, the 1974 Lalonde Report acknowledged that social and physical environments in which people live can affect their health. And the health promotion approach on which this report was based has emphasized societal values and is strongly committed to equity and social justice. Health promotion activists also have long experience in mobilizing community action to address inequalities in health.

Social and environmental determinants were also acknowledged in the preamble to the 1984 Canada Health Act, which outlined the interconnections between the various elements that influence health — although the emphasis seemed to be predominantly on lifestyles. "Canadians can achieve further improvements in their well-being," said the preamble, "through combining individual lifestyles that emphasize fitness, prevention, and health promotion with collective action against the social, environmental, and occupational causes of disease, and they desire a system of health services that will promote such physical and mental health and such protection against disease."

As health policy in Canada evolved from a strong emphasis on health promotion to focus more on population health, social and economic issues were in the forefront, although it appears there is still no clear vision about how to implement what the Canada Health Act described as "collective action against the social, environmental, and occupational causes of disease."

The new "population health" approach was reflected in the health strategy outlined in a 1994 report called *Strategies for Population Health: Investing in the Health of Canadians.*[17] The report was prepared by the Federal, Provincial and Territorial Advisory Committee on Population Health, and the framework and strategic directions in the discussion paper were adopted by the Federal, Provincial and Territorial Ministers of Health at their September 1994 meeting in Halifax. The strategy claims to encompass "all the major influences on health," including:

- **living and working conditions** (the social and economic environment): income, employment, social status, social support networks, education, and social factors in the workplace;
- **physical environment:** physical factors in the workplace, housing conditions, as well as other aspects of the natural and human-built environment;
- **personal health practices, individual capacity, and coping skills:** behaviours that enhance health or create risks to health, as well as individual characteristics such as coping skills, decision-making skills and human biology; and
- **health services:** services to promote, protect, maintain and restore good health.

The report notes that healthy child development is not included as a separate category in the framework, in spite of its crucial importance as an influence on health. Rather, each of the categories includes factors known to contribute to healthy child development.

The role of the Advisory Committee on Population Health (ACPH) is to advise the Conference of Deputy Ministers of Health on national and interprovincial strategies that could be considered to improve the health status of the Canadian population, and to provide a more integrated approach to health. The members of the advisory committee include officials from federal and provincial health ministries, as well as a number of external representatives.

The ACPH *Report on the Health of Canadians,* prepared for the September 1996 meeting of the Federal, Provincial and Territorial Ministers of Health in Toronto,[18] goes into some detail about the challenges to the health of the population posed by living and working and conditions and physical environment. It says that "Current trends in many of the most powerful factors that make and keep people healthy, such as employment, adequate income, and a fair distribution of wealth, are cause for concern."[19]

Can the health of Canadians be improved and the inequalities in health status be reduced? The report answers unequivocally: yes. But to be successful, it says, the following challenges will have to be met:

Living and working conditions:
- Create a thriving, sustainable economy, with meaningful work for all.
- Ensure an adequate income for all Canadians.
- Reduce the number of families living in poverty.
- Achieve an equitable distribution of income.
- Ensure healthy working conditions.
- Encourage life-long learning.
- Foster friendship and social support networks in families and in communities.

Physical environment:
- Foster a healthy and sustainable environment.

- Ensure suitable, adequate, and affordable housing.
- Create safe and well-designed communities.

Personal Health Practices and Coping Skills:
- Foster healthy child development.
- Encourage healthy life-choice decisions.

Health Services:
- Ensure appropriate and affordable health services, accessible to all.
- Reduce preventable illness, injury, disability, and death.

The magnitude of such a task — particularly in the area of living and working conditions — is evident. The report clearly acknowledges that meeting this wide array of challenges will require a collaborative effort across many sectors, as well as the active support of the general public. The health sector cannot act alone, the report notes, since most of the factors influencing health fall outside its purview. It suggests that the next step towards improving the overall health of Canadians would be to develop national health goals.

The politics of population health

It seems clear that the socioeconomic factors which make and keep people healthy, and which the health ministers identified as "cause for concern," would need to be addressed by economic and social policies. But in spite of their clear listing of what would be required, making a serious attempt to address these socioeconomic factors as a key priority in "population health" policies has not yet been incorporated into strategies to improve the health of the population.

It is also important to note that, while those concerned about health have clearly identified social and economic conditions as key determinants of health, the evolution of health policy emphasis from "health promotion" to "population health" has generated considerable controversy. Hayes and Dunn point out that, by focusing on social structure, the population health approach "provided important ammunition to advocates of the welfare state, who were under siege at this time [the early 1990s] in the climate of deficit reduction and neo-conservative economic evangelism."[20] But, at the same time, as these authors also note, claims made by the CIAR population health group that "health care has relatively little impact on health status (or at least less impact than other forms of investment or activity) and that sustained economic growth is essential to improving overall levels of health status, likely also appealed to neo-conservative sensibilities and interests."

The CIAR seems to have been the main driving force behind the population health approach in Canada. And, as Hayes and Dunn point out, the CIAR "started as an élite group of researchers inspired largely by one person's vision, and significantly financed through corporate sponsorship. It has never had a strong community development component as part of its organizing logic." Its primary organizational purpose has been the assembly and interpretation of evidence.[21] Of course, the way in which that activity has been conducted reflects the particular bias of those who undertake the work. Population health, as Hayes and Dunn point out, is neither value neutral nor ideologically innocent — regardless of what is advocated in its name.

The population health approach recognizes social structure is crucial in shaping health and well-being. It also moves beyond a preoccupation with individual biology or personal choice. But the absence of a theoretical framework for the "population health" approach is a serious concern — particularly in relation to the socioeconomic determinants of health.

In a recent critique of a CIAR paper on *The Determinants of Health,*[22] Michael Hayes points out that "By demonstrating links between income and health and unemployment and health, the population health approach suggested that social structure, and not merely individual behaviour, be an important focus of the analysis."

But presenting evidence of the impact of socioeconomic inequality in health status apparently has not led authors currently working in the field of population health to challenge the underlying social and economic structure directly. Several observers have also noted that the population health approach generally ignores the impact of gender in socioeconomic inequalities as they relate to health. And other critics of the CIAR work on the determinants of health note that it generally also ignores race and power relationships. To the extent that inequalities are mentioned, there is little or no analysis of their causes, says another critic.[23]

In their 1998 CPRN paper, Hayes and Dunn observe that the epistemological base of the CIAR methodology "did not readily embrace practices from the social sciences — use of narrative and individual experience (qualitative methods) application/integration of contemporary social theory within framework, objectivity/subjectivity position of research as action, development of notions of power, identity, gender, communication, or analysis of labour or land markets, the space economy, and so forth."[24]

However, according to Hayes and Dunn, these themes are increasingly being broached by the group as the circle of researchers involved in the analysis expands and the link to a medical school on the part of group members becomes weaker. The approach of some CIAR researchers who claim that "data unite, theories divide," may reflect the organizational necessity of "sticking to the facts," according to Hayes and Dunn, even though any empirical analysis involves theorization (however implicit), and even "facts" are not value free.

It must be emphasized that the population health framework has specific implications for public policy that are not politically or ideologically neutral, these authors say. "Many dimensions of social relations are simultaneously involved in shaping our health experiences — global capitalism, gender, ethnicity, religion, identity, power, housing, telecommunications...topics that have been traditionally under-theorized (i.e., treated as numerical variables, acknowledged as important without explications as to how or why they are so, or ignored altogether) within epidemiologic research."[25]

However, a 1996 book by British author Richard G. Wilkinson, *Unhealthy Societies: the Afflictions of Inequality,*[26] marks one of the first attempts to establish a theoretical framework for the population health debate. In *Unhealthy Societies,* Wilkinson argues for a "societal approach to health," and explains why this is important. Studies of individuals and social groups typically come up with sharply contrasting policy implications, he says. This approach tries to identify people with symptoms of some disease or social problem and then find out what is — or was — different about their lifestyle or socioeconomic circumstances. Almost invariably, he says, the result is that you identify a group of people 'at high risk' of the disease, because they have some particular vulnerability factors, and the problem then becomes how to intervene among this group to prevent them getting the disease.

This applies not just to health, says Wilkinson, but also to studies of a wide range of social, psychological, developmental and educational problems. Expensive new services may then be proposed to cater to the individuals most affected, but meanwhile the original source of the problem in society is left unchanged. In terms of research, says Wilkinson, "the explana-

Health and Wealth

tions of what makes whole populations healthier than others may be very different from the evidence of what makes some individuals healthier than others."

Wilkinson argues that healthy, egalitarian societies are more socially cohesive. They have a stronger community life and suffer fewer of the corrosive effects of inequality. The public arena becomes a source of supportive social networks, rather than of stress and potential conflict. Improvements to health will only come by changing social structure to increase equity.

"Healthy public policies"

The implication of a "population health" approach to health policy is that policies to improve population health may now have to include policies to address living and working conditions and the physical environment, as well as the more traditional health policy concerns such as personal health practices or "lifestyles" and health services. But policy-makers do not seem ready to pursue the "population health" approach to its logical conclusion. Meanwhile, confusion between health promotion and population health seems to continue.

In a February 1996 paper on *Population Health Promotion* for the Health Promotion and Development Division of Health Canada, Nancy Hamilton and Tariq Bhatti noted that "many are asking how population health and health promotion are related." Many people think that population health is no different from public health and community health, these authors say. Some people believe that it is a new paradigm, while others believe that the concepts and principles of population health and health promotion are essentially the same.

But their 1996 paper sidesteps the issue of distinguishing between the two approaches. They say that, "Rather than engage in a debate over the similarities and differences between a 'health promotion' and a 'population health' approach," they will combine the ideas to provide "an integrated Population Health Promotion Model."

Hamilton and Bhatti explain that their model for population health promotion "draws on a **population health** approach by showing that, in order to improve the health of the people, action must be taken on the full range of health determinants." But they add that "the model draws on **health promotion** by showing that comprehensive action strategies are needed to influence the underlying factors and conditions that determine health."

As these authors also note, Canada's strategy for population health acknowledges that "it is not the amount of wealth, but its relative distribution, which is the key factor that determines health status. Likewise, social status affects people by determining the degree of control people have over life circumstances and hence, their capacity to take action."[27]

It would appear that, if action is to be taken on "the full range of health determinants," including socioeconomic factors, a comprehensive and concerted strategy will be needed. In its 1994 document, *Strategies for Population Health: Investing in the Health of Canadians*, the ACPH proposed that these problems should be attacked through "healthy public policies." It is not entirely clear how that term was to be interpreted. Hamilton and Bhatti seem to suggest such policies might include anything from "healthier choices of goods and services"[28] to "equitable distribution of income." But it seems clear that a concerted effort to address the inequitable distribution of income as a way to improve the overall health of the population is not yet on the policy agenda in Canada.

In fact, the emphasis on "healthy public policy" as a way of addressing the socioeconomic and other determinants of health reflects a world-wide movement being promoted by the WHO.

Skeptics have described "healthy public policy" as "a political agenda of reforms from the 1960s"[29] which seeks "the redistribution of power through wider participation in the decisions that determine the conditions of modern life."

According to political scientist Theodore Marmor, Professor of Public Policy and Management at Yale University, "At best, 'healthy public policy' represents modern Utopianism. At worst, it is simply a form of clever propaganda, piggybacking a set of other policy interests onto the powerful and broadly-based public support for health."[30] In its extreme form, says Marmor, the "healthy public policy" approach "detaches the concept of 'health' from any of its conventional and (potentially) objectively measurable manifestations, and declares that health is whatever the people (which ones?) declare it to be. If the state has a legitimate interest in, and indeed an obligation to promote 'health,' then surely it must support these local initiatives."[31]

It seems apparent that a "healthy public policy" approach is not intended to challenge the fundamental basis of poverty, unemployment or income distribution, which are major determinants of population health. As critics of U.S. federal policies to promote healthy workplaces have pointed out, "What remained unchallenged was the basic governance of the workplace and the legitimacy of the present distribution of income, power and status that work largely determines."[32]

Willingness to challenge those entrenched structures is considerably risky, as the British Working Group on Health Inequalities discovered. The release of its report in 1980 caused an uproar. The Black Report concluded that the predominant or governing explanation for inequalities in health lay in material deprivation. It recommended radical improvements in the life of poorer groups, especially children and people with disabilities, by increasing or introducing cash benefits, e.g., a child benefit, maternity grant and infant care allowance, and a comprehensive disablement allowance, and developing new schemes for day nurseries, ante-natal clinics, sheltered housing, home improvements, improved conditions at work, and community services.[33] The report was rejected by the newly-elected Conservative government, which refused to print or distribute the report and circulated only a limited number of photocopies without issuing a press release or holding a press conference.

A follow-up report, *The Health Divide,* by Margaret Whitehead,[34] who had been asked to update the findings of the Black Report, caused a similar furore when it was released in 1986. Attempts were made in the House of Commons to discredit both reports. And a former Conservative Secretary of State for Health claimed that both reports were "Marxist" and showed a "fascination with a class division of society which is basically a Marxist approach."[35]

A number of government ministers, while conceding that health differences existed, said they were a function of "lifestyle choices" and not of poverty or deprivation.

In Canada, as in most industrial societies — particularly where health care is publicly funded — health policy has focused on the health care system itself. Sociologist Marc Renaud, a vice-president of the CIAR and professor of sociology at the University of Montreal, points out that the health policy debate generally focuses unilaterally on the legitimacy of the financial demands made on the health care system by physicians, hospitals, other participants, and sometimes by specific groups of beneficiaries. The main issue should now be the re-orientation and refocusing of the social debate, he says.

"The scope, organization, and financing of the various social security regimes (medical care insurance, old age pensions, unemployment benefits, etc.) have to be re-examined with one central, yet often forgotten question in mind: What reforms would help improve the health of the population?"[36]

Action to address the socioeconomic determinants of the health of the population may be even more difficult than that. In *Unhealthy Societies*, Richard Wilkinson takes the analysis further. His work is based on the premise that social cohesion is crucial to the quality of life. Increased inequality, he says, imposes a psychological burden which reduces the well-being of the whole society. The pattern of modern disease shows that the material standard of living in developed countries is no longer the main issue. The problem now is the psycho-social quality of life, which must be supported by greater material equality. Without it, he says, important social needs will go unmet and health will suffer.

Chapter 2
INEQUALITIES IN HEALTH

It is widely acknowledged that socioeconomic factors are key elements in the health of populations and can result in inequalities in health between different groups and segments of the population. There is now a very extensive world-wide literature on health inequalities and the socioeconomic factors that are responsible for them. There also appears to be a general agreement that societies concerned with improving the health of their populations will have to make efforts to address the socioeconomic factors that influence health.

In Canada, for example, the Board of Directors of the Canadian Public Health Association (CPHA) issued a comprehensive discussion paper on *Health Impacts of Social and Economic Conditions: Implications for Public Policy* in March 1997.[1] In early 1995, the CPHA Board had identified health impacts of social and economic conditions and policies as a priority for action within the Association. It established a Working Group that brought together individuals working in social and economic policy development who had a broad range of experience in examining social and economic conditions in Canada to develop the discussion paper.

The paper explores various dimensions of the socioeconomic environment, including income distribution, education, unemployment, systemic discrimination, and violence. It identifies the health impacts of these factors and considers policy implications. The CPHA says these include changes to income programs and taxes, labour legislation, education and training programs, and social supports and services.

The ACPH *Report on the Health of Canadians,* prepared for the September 1996 meeting of the Federal, Provincial and Territorial Ministers of Health,[2] also discussed how the health of the population might be improved by addressing the challenges posed by living and working conditions and physical environments, among other things. This report notes that health is greatly affected by things in our social and economic environment, such as having an adequate income, physical safety, learning opportunities, and meaningful work. Friendship and other support networks in our families, workplaces and communities, and social roles, such as the roles of women and men in society, also have an important impact. In fact, says this report, "evidence suggests that living and working conditions are perhaps the most powerful influences on health."[3]

International bodies such as the World Health Organization have recognized the importance of socioeconomic trends for the health of societies. In setting out a common framework for countries to implement the strategy of health for all by the year 2000, the WHO urged countries to review economic trends, in part "to help identify health risks related to adverse economic conditions."[4]

The WHO 1996 common framework was actually the third version it has published. The first was developed in 1982. The WHO says that this third version was designed to induce and support analytical rather than "merely descriptive review." Among the questions it suggests countries might ask are these:

- What are the trends in employment and unemployment, and are there identifiable groups which have become or are becoming disenfranchised?

- Are government revenues sufficient to sustain an adequate level of public expenditure?
- How is the country's wealth spread throughout the population?
- Are the underprivileged groups concentrated in rural areas or is poverty an urban feature (and to what extent)? The national average could conceal an unbalanced distribution of income which affects the health status of the poorest population groups.
- Are the economic prospects expected to improve the present distribution of income?
- If structural adjustment policies have been necessary, what has been their impact?
- Have the effects of unemployment had an influence on income distribution, and how is this situation changing?

The section of the WHO framework document dealing with social trends notes that, "Often, social protection has broken down and joblessness and the social exclusion of significant portions of the population have become a reality."[5] It suggests key elements in the area of social trends might be education, employment, the role of women, social exclusion, technology and communications. Priority should be given to these areas to determine current trends and their impact on health. On the question of social exclusion, the framework document asks countries to consider these questions:

- Are significant sectors of the society excluded, because of age, sex, education, race, ethnic identity, or for other reasons, from full participation in the life of the society, including equitable access to employment, social protection, education, and life-chances?

- To what extent is this situation affecting health status within the country as a whole and for the specific groups?

The WHO asked countries to comment on the nature of political, economic, demographic, and social trends that have affected and influenced health and health development since the second evaluation (in 1991). While its document is intended as a guide, it also notes that most countries have adapted the guidelines to their own situation and developed national strategies and objectives for the attainment of health by the year 2000.

In Canada, the influence of social environment on health was recognized by the government as early as 1974 in the Lalonde report, *A New Perspective on the Health of Canadians*.[6] More recent reports, such as the *Report on the Health of Canadians*,[7] have devoted considerable attention to living and working conditions and the physical environment. This report, which was intended "to inform Canadians about the state of their health and the major factors that influence health," notes that Canada's overall standard of health is not shared equally by all sectors in Canadian society. There are differences in health status by age, sex, level of income, education, and geographic area. This is how the findings of the report are summarized:

- **Age differences.** While physical health and functional ability decline with age, there is more stress and depression among the young than among the older population. Psychological well-being and job satisfaction are also rated better among those who are older.
- **Male-Female Differences.** By many measures, women are healthier than men. On average, women live about six years longer than men, and they enjoy more years free of dis-

abling health problems. However, in recent years, the gap in longevity has been closing. This appears to be related to increasing smoking rates among women and improved health behaviours among men (less risk behaviours such as drunk driving and smoking).

On measures such as self-rated health, psychological well-being, stress, and depression, women do not score as well as men, on average. The reasons for these male-female differences are not known precisely.

- **Living and Working Conditions.** The rich are healthier than the middle class, who are in turn healthier than the poor. The well-educated are healthier than the less-educated, and the employed are healthier than the unemployed.

Income, education, and employment are all indicators of living and working conditions, says the report. These factors affect health by themselves, but also interact with each other. The combined factors of chronic unemployment, inadequate education, inadequate nutrition, and poor housing all contribute to the generally poor level of health experienced by many Aboriginal communities, and by both working and unemployed poor throughout Canada.

- **Provincial Differences.** The report notes that on most health status indicators, there are very large contrasts in overall population health among the provinces and territories. In some cases, the difference is two-fold or more between the first-ranked and last-ranked province.

The report, which was also seen as a first step toward implementing some of the strategies outlined in the ACPH's

1994 document *Strategies for Population Health: Investing in the Health of Canadians,*[8] goes into some detail about a range of different measures of health, many of which relate to disease, health conditions, life expectancy, and death rates. But it also links health to some socioeconomic factors such as education, income and social status, and provides some analysis of these links.

Commenting on the relationship of health to living and working conditions, the *Report on the Health of Canadians* notes that "these well-known relationships are found in Canada, as in virtually every other society."[9] However, the analysis of the relationship between socioeconomic factors and health is limited to two or three key areas: income, social status, and education. Other sections of the report describe trends in various key variables, such as levels of education, rates of low income, unemployment, income inequality, and the size of the middle class, but no attempt is made to track the health impact of these trends over time.

It is clear that further analysis is needed to determine the impact on the health of the Canadian population of trends in literacy, low income, and so on. Longitudinal data, where available, would help in documenting the extent to which trends in these key socioeconomic variables have affected the health of the Canadian population. For example, the report notes that, compared with most other developed countries, Canada has a very high poverty rate, particularly among single-parent families. But no information is presented to indicate how this has affected the health of the Canadian population in comparison with the population of other developed countries.

Canada's health status is compared with that of other countries, using key measures such as life expectancy at birth, infant death rates, low birth-weight rates, and the rate of AIDS infections. But it is not clear how trends in these indicators are linked to trends in the socioeconomic variables described elsewhere in the report. On many health indicators, Japan and Sweden are said to have achieved "the best rates in the world." And, according to the report, these two countries "provide a convenient gold standard or benchmark for measuring Canada's level of health."[10]

Wilkinson attributes the success of Japan to "the association of a narrow income distribution with a public sphere of life which has a real social content."[11] He notes that what Sweden and Japan have in common is a much more egalitarian distribution of income — although he also emphasizes that, where family structure is concerned, "they are at opposite ends of the spectrum."[12]

However, other analysts have pointed out that Japan's economic development, health status indicators, and state funding of health care are used to argue that it is possible to spend less on health care and obtain higher levels of health status through continued and sustained economic growth. But they also note that this interpretation hides many important points — the significant portion of health care that is provided privately in Japan; the cultural "costs" of this (especially to women, the main care-givers in a patriarchal society); the relationship between corporations and workers in which corporations make a long-term commitment to workers; the environmental costs to other countries of Japanese investment; and the role of "distant strangers" in the economic "success" story.[13] It is obvious that simple comparisons between countries or between segments of the population within a country do not always tell the whole story.

While the *Report on the Health of Canadians* acknowledges that there are difficulties in collecting comparable statistics between countries, it presents a few key indicators, such as Gross Domestic Product (GDP) per capita, rates of child poverty, adult literacy rates, and unemployment rates. However, what seems to be missing is any discussion of how these differences might relate to health differences between countries.

For example, according to the report, among industrialized countries, Finland and Sweden have the most equitable distribution of wealth. Canada has more income inequality than most developed countries, although less than Australia. Do these differences translate into similar differences in population health between the countries named? The report does not say. It does, however, reproduce a ranking of various countries according to the United Nations Human Development Index (HDI), without discussing whether or not this is an appropriate measure of the health of the populations of the countries included.

The construction of indicators of well-being, or population health, may in itself be biased because of the variables selected or excluded from a particular indicator. And the United Nations HDI includes only three variables: life expectancy, educational attainment and per capita income. But it is clear that some sort of measurement tools are needed by policymakers wishing to improve population health by addressing some of the socioeconomic factors that may determine health. (Indicators of social health and well-being, as well as the establishment of benchmarks as policy goals, are discussed in the next chapter of this report.)

While it is generally accepted that socioeconomic factors such as poverty, unemployment, housing, early childhood development and income distribution have an important bearing on the health of populations, there appears to be only limited work to date that looks at how trends in these variables in Canada have affected the overall health of the Canadian population. The 1996 *Report on the Health of Canadians* reviews key socioeconomic factors, and a *Technical Appendix* accompanying the report presents more details of the data used, as well as charts plotting the trends identified.[14] But the report, except in one or two key areas, does not really attempt to answer the WHO question: "To what extent is this situation affecting health status within the country as a whole and for the specific groups?"

Income and Social Status

According to the *Report on the Health of Canadians*, higher incomes are related to better health, not only because of the ability to purchase adequate housing, food, and other basic necessities. A higher income also means more choices and a feeling that people have more control over their lives. That feeling of being in control is basic to good health.

This was one of the key findings of the famous Whitehall Study of British civil servants, begun in 1967.[15] The study showed a steep inverse association between social class, assessed by grade of employment, and mortality from a wide range of diseases. After ten years of follow-up, those in the highest grades of employment had about one-third the mortality rate of those in the lowest grades. This difference in mortality was only partly explained by differences in age, smoking, systolic blood pressure, height, plasma cholesterol and blood glucose. Based on the limited data available, there were also substantial socioeconomic differences in morbidity.[16]

Death rates were three times as high among the most junior office support staff as they were among the senior administrators. It is important to note that the people being studied were all white-collar workers who worked together in the same offices. Many people had thought that differences in health related to social class or economic status would not be apparent in such a relatively homogenous group. The participants in the study were in stable employment, and they lived and worked in one part of the country.[17]

They were also all men — an important limitation that has been noted by critics of the study, who have also pointed out that family composition was not taken into account, either.[18] Such factors could have a significant bearing on the outcome. In fact, it would appear that the majority of studies that relate socioeconomic factors to health are based on males only. Studies like the first Whitehall study, which are often described as "gender neutral," in fact ignore gender differences which may be significant for the results of the research. It was perhaps with unintended irony that the chapter on "The Social and Cultural Matrix of Health and Disease" in the Canadian Institute of Advanced Research's landmark book *Why Are Some People Healthy and Others Not?* begins with a section headed "No man is an island."[19] We will return later to gender bias in research on socioeconomic determinants of health.

In the Whitehall study, control over work was significantly related to health, even after controlling for employment grade and a number of other risk factors. Conflicting job demands and, in the absence of control, a heavy workload, were also associated with poorer health in this study.

A second longitudinal study, conducted between 1985 and 1988, included women and confirmed the results of the first study. The Whitehall II study found that men and women in the lowest grade of the civil service had six times more sick leave, both short spells and longer absences, than men and women in the highest grade. Michael Marmot, one of the authors of the study, notes that none of those who participated could be considered poor by any absolute standard. The problem was therefore not simply one of explaining the link between poverty and ill-health, but of understanding the reason for the social gradient.

If every social group had the mortality rates of the group at the top, says Marmot, there would be a marked improvement in public health — for example, life expectancy at age 45 for lower-grade civil servants would be extended by four years. "If we understood the reasons for the inequity," he says, "we might be able to so something about the problem."[20]

In Canada, the first major analysis of social status and health was completed in 1938.[21] Marsh, Grant and Blackler conducted a number of surveys focusing on the health experiences of employed and unemployed workers and their families, and found that various health problems were more prevalent among the unemployed. They identified underweight and malnutrition, decayed teeth and infected gums, rates of deafness and other auditory defects, and abnormal conditions of the nose and throat. These authors concluded that, while the situation could be improved by the availability of medical services, unless the prior social conditions giving rise to these inequalities were improved, social status differences in health would remain.[22]

A number of studies on the subject of the impact of income and social status on health are reviewed in a 1993 paper by David Hay for the Social Development Research Program of the Social Planning and Research Council of British Columbia, *Does Money Buy Health?*[23] Hay's analysis, based on 1977 data, found that low-income groups have poorer health status than other income groups; older respondents have poorer health status than younger respondents; but low- income groups have poorer health at all ages; women have poorer health status than men, but lower income is related to poorer health for both men and women; change in income status is causal of change in health status; and the relationships between income and health are partially explained or interpreted through the influence of income on a variety of 'intermediate' social variables.[24]

Hay also concluded that, while it is evident that lower social status is related to lower health status, a better understanding of the mechanisms operating in this relationship is still needed.[25]

The 1996 *Report on the Health of Canadians,* in its analysis of the link between health and income and social status, cited a study by Russell Wilkins of *Mortality by neighbourhood income in urban Canada,*[26] and noted that Canadians in the highest income bracket live longer than those in the bottom bracket. About 50% of men living in the poorest neighbourhoods will live to age 75, while almost 70% of men from the richest neighbourhoods will reach this age. The study found that the relationship between health and income is not just a matter of being very rich or very poor. There is also a gradient in health status, such that health increases at each step of the hierarchy in income, education, or social status.

A gap between the rich and poor exists for most types of illnesses and for almost all causes of death, according to this study. In other words, the poor — and other groups suffering from high death rates — do not suffer more from any one disease or a few particular diseases. Rather, people who are living at a socioeconomic disadvantage are biologically more susceptible to becoming sick and dying.

The *Report on the Health of Canadians* suggests these findings may be surprising to some. "After all," says the report, "we have a health system that provides almost equal access to care for all Canadians, regardless of their income. Even after several decades of Medicare, inequalities in health status within our society still persist." This provides further evidence, says the report, that health services are not the only — or even the most important — influence on health.

The 1980 Black Report on health inequalities in Britain came to exactly the same conclusion. The solution to high mortality rates among the poor, said this report, lay outside the National Health Service.[27] Indeed, the *Report on the Health of Canadians* acknowledges that efforts to improve health, given the recognition that health is influenced by many factors other than health care, will require the cooperation of many ministries, both federal and provincial, including health, finance, education, social services, housing, labour, justice, aboriginal affairs, and economic development.[28]

It is interesting to note that Canadian researchers Marsh, Grant and Blackler, in their analysis of *Health and Unemployment* — published almost 60 years earlier in 1938 — also emphasized the importance of addressing underlying socioeconomic inequalities if real improvements in the health of the Canadian population are to be achieved.

Education and literacy

The 1996 *Report on the Health of Canadians* noted that health status improves with one's level of education. From a specially commissioned micro-data analysis, based on data from Statistics Canada's National Population Health Survey of 1994-95,[29] the report concludes that, on average, as education increases, self-rated health status improves, while activity limitation and the number of work-days lost due to illness or injury decrease. Those with a university degree are about half as likely to have high blood pressure, high blood cholesterol, or to be overweight, as are those with less than high school education.

As the report points out, a person's education, occupation and income are all indicators or markers of his or her living and working conditions. These markers are closely related, because on average people with higher levels of education are more likely to be employed, to have jobs with higher social status, and to have stable incomes.

The CPHA report also notes that low literacy skills are also associated with poor health.[30] Low literacy can affect health directly — for example, through misreading prescriptions. Much of the available health education literature requires a level of reading ability that makes it inaccessible to a large proportion of the population in greatest need of health information, says the CPHA. But psychosocial effects linked with low literacy skills include stress and diminished self-confidence.

Low self-esteem often makes it difficult to seek employment or to socialize. Workers with poor literacy skills are particularly vulnerable to lay-off and, once unemployed, may find it difficult to find new jobs. As many as 42% of all Canadians have weak reading skills and approximately the same proportion has difficulty reading documents and performing arithmetic functions.[31]

A 1995 survey of adult literacy placed Canada in the second tier of tested countries, along with the Netherlands, Germany and the United States. The survey found strong links in all countries between literacy skills, employment and occupational status.[32]

Data from the 1996 census, released in April 1998, show some improvement in the educational level of Canadians over the past 15 years. For instance, in 1996, graduates from university or other post-secondary institutions represented 40% of the population aged 15 and over, compared with just 29% in 1981. On the other hand, 35% of the population aged 15 and over had not completed high school, down from 48% in 1981.[33] But the unemployment rate for those who had not completed high school had worsened since 1981. For example, between 1981 and 1996, the unemployment rate for persons aged 25 to 34 with less than high school education increased from 10% to 18%.

Health and Wealth

The rate for those who had completed university rose from 3.3% to 4.6%.[34]

Early childhood development and child poverty

The impact of early childhood development on long-term health is now well-established. The Canadian Institute for Advanced Research, for example, has undertaken considerable work in this area. Fraser Mustard and John Frank, in a 1991 paper on *The Determinants of Health*,[35] note that there is now evidence that how children are cared for at an early age can influence their coping skills — and by association their health — for the rest of their childhood and their entire life. They cite a number of studies to demonstrate this, including one randomized controlled trial of a pre-school enrichment program in an inner city ghetto in the United States: the well-known Perry Pre-school Program. A 19-year follow-up demonstrated that the intervention group did better than the control group in the following respects: a higher proportion graduated from high school and went on to college; less than half as many were ever classified as having mental disabilities; 40% fewer were on welfare; and teen-age pregnancies among the female subjects occurred at half the rate of the controlled group.

Research shows that social class differences in intellectual development are evident very early in life, and that lower socioeconomic groups are particularly sensitive to the impacts of parental stress.[36] Prolonged stress can seriously impair the immune system, and long-term stress can also cause permanent damage to brain function, including learning and memory. The good news, as the CPHA notes in its 1997 paper on *Health Impacts of Social and Economic Conditions: Implications for Public Policy*, is that animal studies show early nurturing can provide long-term protection against such effects later in life.[37]

The CPHA cites other studies that have shown physiological links between external stimuli and the development of the neural system, which have profound implications for health. Animal studies have also shown that the quality of the sensory information provided to an animal during its early stages can have a profound impact on how the nervous system develops. An information-rich early environment affects neural development positively, better equipping the organism for later life and life-long learning.[38]

Work by David Barker in the United Kingdom demonstrated strong links between low birth-weight and incidence of heart disease in the subjects almost 50 years later. Again, these studies focused on men only, but they have aroused considerable interest and some controversy. In a 1995 paper for the CIAR, Frank says "it is still unclear how much this correlation simply represents the tracking of persistent socioeconomic exposures and experiences inside a society with relatively rigid barriers to upward mobility." But he suggests Barker's work is worthy of further attention by researchers. "It may simply be that early life characteristics are in fact themselves outcomes of adverse social and economic environments that are by and large maintained throughout life in many societies," says Frank, "leading in turn to premature disease and death later in life."[39]

While some critics of Barker's work have claimed that both low birth-weight and subsequent heart disease risk are themselves associated with poverty, such criticisms only serve to emphasize the serious health impact of poverty, especially on children. For example, the Wilkins study of *Mortality by neighbourhood income in urban Canada*,[40] published in 1995, found that babies born in poor neighbourhoods continue to have a greater risk of death than infants from wealthy neighbourhoods. Although the infant mortality rate declined by half in both poor and rich neighbourhoods between 1971 and 1991, it remained almost twice as high in the poorest neighbourhoods.

Researchers from the Canadian Council on Social Development (CCSD) have emphasized that "The persistence of higher infant mortality rates in poor neighbourhoods clearly demonstrates the life-and-death consequences of income inequality in Canada."[41] In a 1996 report called *Child Poverty: What Are the Consequences?* for the Centre for International Statistics at CCSD, Ross, Scott and Kelly summarize the health consequences of child poverty as follows:

- Poor infants still have a higher mortality rate;
- Low birth-weight is more prevalent in poor neighbourhoods, and there is a well-established link between low birth-weight and significant problems later in life;
- Disability is linked to low income — for example, low income during pregnancy is strongly linked with poor birth outcomes;
- Poor children are more likely to suffer from mental health problems;
- Poor children have lower levels of educational attainment. For example, when compared with non-poor teens, twice as many poor teens aged 16 and 17 drop out before they complete high school. While the number of drop-outs has declined over the past decade, the difference in educational achievement between children from poor and non-poor families has persisted.
- Children in families with low incomes are more likely to live in houses with damp walls and ceilings, crumbling foundations, rotting porches and steps, and corroded pipes. The number of children living under these conditions in-

creased by 21% from 1990 to 1992 as a result of the recession.

- Many poor children live in unsafe housing. Death rates due to accidents are higher in the poorest neighbourhoods in Canada.
- Poor teens are more likely to smoke and to have alcohol problems.
- A health survey in Ontario found that 18% of young women aged 16 to 19 from low-income families had been pregnant in the previous five years, compared with 4% of young women from higher-income families. Young women giving birth in their teens represent a significant risk to their babies and to their own life chances.

According to the 1996 *Report on the Health of Canadians*, child poverty rates in Canada have remained roughly at the same level over the past ten years,[42] with 1.4 million children still living in poverty. But the National Council of Welfare notes that this was, in fact, a 16-year high.[43] Statistics Canada reported that, in 1994, one child in every five lived in a low-income family. Among lone-parent families headed by women, more than half a million children — three in every five in this group — were in a low-income household.

Even more disturbing is the fact that child poverty rates have continued to rise since the Ministers of Health issued their report, citing 1994 data. By 1996, the percentage of children living in low-income families had risen to 21.1%, substantially above the 15.3% of children who lived in low-income families in 1989. An estimated 1,498,000 children lived in low-income families in 1996, or 47% more than in 1989. During this same period, the total number of children increased by just 7%.[44] The significance of these trends for population health is indeed alarming.

Aboriginal health

The *Report on the Health of Canadians* notes that Canada's Aboriginal people, as a group, are the most disadvantaged of all citizens, and have the poorest overall health status. Although Aboriginal people have made significant health gains in recent years, their life expectancy is still seven years less than that of the overall Canadian population, and there are almost twice as many infant deaths among Aboriginal peoples — a higher rate than the poorest neighbourhoods in urban Canada.[45] (The report notes that these data are based only on the Status Indian population, so may not reflect the health status in all Aboriginal communities, which include non-Status Indian peoples, Inuit peoples, and Métis peoples.)

The CPHA report notes that the lower health status of Aboriginal peoples is reflected in higher rates of infant mortality, injury, tobacco use, and chronic diseases. Poor social conditions — lack of jobs and access to a clean water supply, physical and social isolation, substandard and crowded housing, and a loss of cultural identity — all contribute to poor health, says the CPHA.[46] Morbidity and mortality rates of Canada's Aboriginal populations are high; the mortality rates of both groups exceed those of the least developed countries. The Aboriginal infant mortality rate is almost twice that of the Canadian population, and the mortality rate of Inuit babies is even higher.

The CPHA report notes that in 1991 67% of Aboriginal people 15 years of age and older identified unemployment as a social problem in their community. A 1995 study by Health Canada found links between socioeconomic factors — such as unemployment, illiteracy, multiple forms of abuse, and low housing standards — and solvent abuse. Other studies have found that those living in inadequate housing on reserves often develop asthma or arthritis, and also experience high hospital admissions for pneumonia, burns, intestinal and skin infections and respiratory, skin and eye diseases.[47]

In 1992, according to the government's own estimates, only half the 70,000 housing units on Indian reserves were adequate or suitable for human habitation. And CMHC reported that in 1991 over 63,000 Aboriginal households living in areas off-reserve were in core housing need. The high levels of crowding in remote and northern Aboriginal housing off-reserve reflects extreme housing shortages in these parts of the country.[48]

Data on education from the 1996 census show that Aboriginal people 15 years of age and over continue to have much lower levels of schooling than the non-Aboriginal population, regardless of age group. Over one-half (54%) of the Aboriginal population aged 15 and over had not received a high school diploma, compared with 35% of the non-Aboriginal population. At higher levels of attainment, Statistics Canada reported that 4.5% of Aboriginal people were university graduates, compared with 16% of the non-Aboriginal population.[49] Although Aboriginal people are making gains in educational attainment, they are experiencing little, if any, improvement relative to the non-Aboriginal population.

Housing

Numerous studies have documented the impact of poor housing on health. The Black Report in Britain found that people who live in houses which they own have lower rates of mortality than those who rent their homes from private landlords. And those tenants, in turn, have lower mortality rates than those who are tenants of local authorities.[50]

The report points out that housing tenure is, of course, one possible measure of the accumulation by an individual or family of fixed property or assets. In other words, the type of housing people live in is also closely related to their financial situation. In Canada, the National Council of Welfare's *Poverty Profile 1995*[51] reported that poverty rates were highest for those who rented their homes. For those under 65, 64% of poor families and 88% of all poor unattached individuals were renters. For those 65 and older, 29% of poor families and 65% of poor unattached seniors were renters.[52]

The follow-up to the Black Report, *The Health Divide* by Margaret Whitehead, published in 1988, cites several different British studies that found that people from "bad" housing areas reported poorer health, more long-standing illness, more recent illness, and more symptoms of depression than those living in "good" housing areas.[53]

The 1996 *Report on the Health of Canadians* noted that housing is important to health in several ways. At the most basic level, housing that is safe, warm and dry is a necessity of life. Housing that is cold, damp, crowded, in poor repair, or in an unsafe neighbourhood can contribute directly to disease or injury. A house is also a home, says this report, "a place where people can feel secure, a place to keep things that are important to them, and a place to develop a sense of identity and belonging — all factors that can enhance health."[54]

In addition, the report points out, housing is generally the largest monthly expenditure for most households. If the cost of housing consumes too much of available income, other needs may suffer and people will be subject to stresses and difficult choices about how to allocate their remaining income — again, all factors that have an impact on health. If people have to move around often in search of suitable and affordable housing, it can disrupt social networks and opportunities for social interaction, all of which can have an impact on health.

Some researchers have compared the impact on health of "housing insecurity" with "job insecurity." For example, one study from Britain indicated that the health effects of housing insecurity showed that the number of tenants who went to see their family doctor changed according to whether the local council's threat to demolish their housing estate was "on" or "off."[55]

The Canada Mortgage and Housing Corporation has developed an index of core housing need, which measures housing need in Canada. According to this index, between one-quarter and one-third of renter households, as well as 40% of mother-led lone-parent households, were unable to access suitable, adequate and affordable housing in 1991.[56] Housing needs were greatest in Prince Edward Island, New Brunswick and British Columbia. Nearly 1.2 million low-income Canadians were in core housing need: they were paying more than 30% of their gross household income for shelter, or living in homes that were otherwise inadequate or unsuitable. Although more recent figures have not yet been released, the number is undoubtedly much higher today. In urban areas, the high cost of shelter makes housing unaffordable for many people. To meet the current and anticipated needs of Canada's Aboriginal peoples, at least 9,000 units per year should be built or renovated.[57]

An increasing number of Canadians have no homes at all. It is difficult to say for sure how many people are now homeless in Canada. A 1986 survey by the Canadian Council on Social Development estimated that between 130,000 and 250,000 people did not have homes or had homes that were grossly inadequate. And, according to the Toronto Coalition Against Homelessness, about 25,000 people were homeless in Metropolitan Toronto in 1996, double the number who were homeless in 1984.[58] As well, the face of homelessness is changing, as families with inadequate incomes or shrinking social assistance benefits find they can no longer meet their rental payments. Young people unable to find work are also found in growing numbers in emergency shelters.

The CPHA report notes that the homeless suffer poorer health status on almost any measure. They are more vulnerable to respiratory diseases, bacterial and viral infections, and are likely to suffer from poor circulation in the legs, leading to swollen legs and feet. Frostbite or hypothermia is a serious threat to people living on the streets in Canada.[59] In recent years, homeless people have frozen to death on the streets in several major Canadian cities.

As well, the CPHA observes, homeless families living in temporary shelters can experience special health difficulties. And homelessness in childhood can contribute to forms of ill-health that are not apparent until later years. Health problems faced by homeless people are often exacerbated by the likelihood that health services may not be available to them because they have no fixed address. As well, they may be reluctant to use health services because of the stigma of being homeless. [60]

Unemployment

The 1996 *Report on the Health of Canadians* says that "meaningful work" is one of the key elements in our social and economic environment that affects health. It also notes that, while unemployment rates — like most other economic indicators — fluctuate from time to time, Canada's unemployment rate has remained relatively high compared with other OECD countries.[61] But no attempt was made to track recent trends in the unemployment rate and relate them to overall measures of population health.

At the beginning of the 1990s, Canada's official unemployment rate was 7%. By 1992, it was over 11%. By the end of 1997, it had fallen back to 8.6%, which still represented more than 1.3 million people who were out of work. Young people aged 15-24 accounted for 29% of those people who were unemployed, and the youth unemployment rate in December 1997 was 15.8%.[62] A disturbing trend noted by Statistics Canada is that the number of young people who have never held a job has increased sharply. In fact, the proportion of young people with no job experience jumped from 9.8% in December 1989 to 24.6% in December 1997. Statistics Canada notes that "This may have a 'scarring' effect on youths trying to break the 'no experience, no job — no job, no experience' cycle."[63]

Statistics Canada also reported that, even with the strong drop in the official unemployment rate during 1997 — from 9.7% at the beginning of the year to 8.6% by the end — Canada's jobless rate remains high internationally, especially in comparison with the United States, where the official unemployment rate in February 1998 stood at 4.6%. In Canada, labour force participation rates have fallen, indicating there are still many "discouraged workers" who have left the labour force because they could not find work. There are also many people working part-time who would prefer full-time jobs if they could find them. According to some estimates, when discouraged workers, involuntary part-time workers and under-employed workers are added in, the real unemployment rate in Canada is closer to 17%.[64]

How have these trends affected the health of Canada's population? Given what we know about the impact of unemployment on health, we can only assume that persistent high unemployment must have had — and continues to have — a negative impact on population health. In the past, social programs have mitigated the impact of unemployment by providing income replacement for those who lose their jobs. But policies to reduce the cost of unemployment benefits, now referred to as Employment Insurance, have meant that only 43% of unemployed Canadians are now entitled to benefits. That percentage is expected to drop to only about one-third once fur-

Health and Wealth

ther cuts are implemented through EI legislation that went into effect in January 1997.[65]

The higher entrance requirement and shortened benefit period time have cut benefit payments by $8 to $10 billion a year. Reductions in unemployment insurance benefit rates, enacted through a series of bills passed during the 1990s, have cut the effective replacement rate of EI benefits to as little as 25% of usual weekly earnings for some claimants.[66]

Social assistance rates in some provinces have also been reduced sharply, so that unemployed people who are not entitled to EI benefits, or whose benefits run out before they find another job, may be in dire straits financially. In Ontario, for example, welfare rates for all recipients except the aged and the disabled were cut by 21.6% as of October 1995. And the National Council of Welfare reports that welfare incomes in all provinces are "abysmally low" — in many cases they are only one-fifth to one-third of Statistics Canada's low-income cutoffs, which the Council regards as "poverty lines."[67]

The loss of a job and the likelihood that there may be no way to replace lost earnings will clearly have an impact on health. But there appears to be little or no work that would link these recent developments in Canada to determine what impact they might have had on the overall health of the Canadian population. Studies are needed to answer the questions posed by the WHO in its 1996 common framework: "To what extent is this situation affecting health status within the country as a whole and for the specific groups?" and "Have the effects of unemployment had an influence on income distribution and how is this situation changing?"[68]

There is an extensive literature on the impact of unemployment on health. In a 1996 Discussion Paper on *The Health Impact of Unemployment*, the Canadian Public Health Association reviewed the findings of a number of different studies on this subject.[69] Since the 1970s, the paper notes, many time-series analyses have reported patterns of high total mortality rates following negative economic trends such as rising unemployment. The most common time lag reported between the unemployment event and subsequent mortality changes was between zero and five years, with time lags most often being between two and three years. Studies have also suggested that mortality is influenced by chronically high (as well as recently rising) unemployment.

The paper suggests that the apparent association of unemployment with total mortality may be better understood by investigating disease-specific causes of death. The most commonly studied specific causes were cardiovascular diseases — especially coronary heart disease — and suicide. Researchers have long been studying the role of stress as a risk factor for cardiac disease and hypertension, and there has been considerable interest in psychological research on the effects of stressful life events, such as the loss of a job. Six aggregate-level analyses, reviewed in the CPHA Paper, reported positive time-series associations between unemployment and heart disease mortality. In fact, the editor of the British Medical Journal is quoted as commenting that "the evidence that unemployment kills — particularly the middle-aged — now verges on the irrefutable."[70]

Other studies have reported that significantly more of those who commit or attempt suicide had been unemployed. Unemployment has also been associated with higher rates of traffic fatalities; with harmful effects on mental and physical health; and with increased use of health care services, through visits to physicians.

All of the studies reviewed concluded that physicians, especially in primary care, could expect higher volumes of patients during hard economic times. Interestingly, one study noted that, in contrast to Britain and Canada, hard times in the United States result in "nearly empty waiting rooms" for most physicians, since joblessness means there are fewer people with either health insurance or the ability to pay cash.[71]

The CPHA Paper points out that questions often arise as to whether unemployment is the cause or the result of ill-health. Many authors have suggested mechanisms of causation, says the paper, but further research is needed to test these hypotheses. In any event, as one recent paper points out, "The general hypothesis for all unemployment-health research is that the change in unemployment rate is positively correlated with changes in adverse health outcomes."[72] According to this paper, evidence of the unemployment-mortality link has been consistent through many studies undertaken in a range of different countries, including Britain, Italy, Finland and Denmark. Research evidence documents the impact of unemployment at both the individual level and at the aggregate level, where studies may look at national data and search for correlations between economic and health indicators (time-series analysis). The authors of this paper advocate that policy-makers be advised about the health consequences "when they pursue policies that, inadvertently or not, increase joblessness."[73]

The lack of a gender analysis

The lack of any gender analysis in the literature on the health impacts of unemployment is striking. Almost all the studies reviewed in the CPHA Paper on *The Health Impact of Unemployment*, for example, are based on male workers only. In some cases, conclusions about the impact of unemployment on mortality rates or other health indicators, based on these males-only studies, are then generalized as applying to the entire work force, ignoring the fact that women now account for a significant percentage of those in paid employment. In

Canada, for example, women constitute more than 45% of the labour force.[74]

Some researchers have claimed that it was too difficult to study women who lost their jobs, because it was hard to know how many women were in the official labour force, how many were actively seeking work, and how many had left the work force or had never entered it because of discouragement.[75] Such rationales for excluding almost half the work force from study are clearly not acceptable, especially given the fact that, at least in Canada, the variables listed are included in the Labour Force Survey for both female and male workers.

Some researchers have suggested that the impact of unemployment on the health of women has been largely ignored because, historically, paid work was assumed to be "less important" for women than for men.[76] This rationale is no longer acceptable, either, given the contribution that women in paid employment make to family income. For example, Statistics Canada reports that in 1992 the earnings of wives in dual-earner families represented 31% of family income, up from 29% in 1989 and 26% in 1967.[77] The most recent labour force data indicate that, among prime-age workers in the age group 25 to 54, 77% of women compared with 91% of men participate in the paid labour force.[78]

In a 1994 paper on *The Health Impact of Unemployment: A Review and Application of Research Evidence*,[79] Lin, Shah and Svoboda say that women who do work outside the home are more likely, compared to men, to be laid off, to fail to be re-employed, to lose more income, and to be single parents with dependents. And a 1986 study, based on data from the Canada Health Survey, found that, controlling for other factors, unemployed females had, on average, worse levels of anxiety, depression and self-rated health status, and made more visits to physicians, than did unemployed males.[80] Lin, Shah and

Svoboda say that "The impact of joblessness on women's health is an imperative research and policy issue." According to these authors, cross-sectional evidence is strong showing that unemployed women suffer as much as men do, but more longitudinal studies on women are needed.

Important as it is to undertake studies of the impact of unemployment on women workers as individuals, it is also important to explore how unemployment of both women and men can affect the overall health of the Canadian population. Indicators of social health and well-being, for example, frequently ignore gender differences. By presenting information as "gender neutral" or "gender blind," researchers often miss differences between women and men that may be crucial for understanding the overall impact of trends. In fact, such research might more appropriately be labeled "gender invisible." We will return to this issue in the next chapter.

Women have sometimes been studied as the spouses of unemployed men. And in some studies of the health impact of unemployment, wives in such situations reported stress-related physical and emotional symptoms similar to those reported by their spouses.[81] There do not appear to be any studies of how the health of men is affected by the unemployment of their wives or partners.

Of course, many women work without pay in their homes as care-givers, and in their communities as volunteers. Many of these women also hold down jobs in the paid work force. Women's unpaid work may expand as services previously provided through the public sector are cut back and as an aging population places an increasing burden on unpaid care-givers. Studies have also documented how the unpaid work of women — and sometimes also their paid work — expands when their spouses or partners are unemployed.[82] The Elliot Lake Tracking Study, supported by Human Resources Development

Canada, is currently examining the impact of mass lay-offs on workers, families and communities. And it has found evidence that women's unpaid work in the home expands to make up for shortfalls in income.[83]

Public policy now seems to expect that paid public services can be replaced by transferring them to the "voluntary sector," where family members (almost always women) will provide them free of charge. Such increases in women's unpaid work — especially at a time when the vast majority of women are also employed in the paid labour force — are bound to have an impact on women's health. This is also an area where more study is needed.

The Federal, Provincial and Territorial Advisory Committee on Population Health, in its 1996 *Report on the Health of Canadians*, said that gender differences in health was one of the topics under consideration for future reports. The Committee should be urged to expand its inquiries to include health impacts of both women's paid and unpaid work and of the changing role of women in society, especially as public services are privatized and pressure on the "voluntary sector" is intensified.

Poverty and income distribution

The common theme running through almost all the socioeconomic issues discussed so far in this Chapter is that of poverty or material deprivation. We know that the rich are healthier than the middle class, who are in turn healthier than the poor. We have seen that higher incomes are related to better health, not only because of the ability to purchase adequate housing, food, and other basic necessities, but also because a higher income means more choices and a feeling that people have more control over their lives and that a feeling of being in control is basic to good health.

We know that — at least as far as men are concerned — Canadians in the highest income bracket live longer than those in the bottom bracket. A gap between the rich and poor exists for most types of illnesses and for almost all causes of death. People who are living at a socioeconomic disadvantage are biologically more susceptible to becoming sick and dying.

We have seen how the health of children who grow up in poor families can be impaired for life, and how the health impact of growing up poor can affect the ability to learn and to develop into healthy, productive adults. We have seen clear evidence of the life-and-death consequences of income inequality in Canada in the persistence of higher infant mortality rates in poor neighbourhoods.

We are also aware that Aboriginal people, as a group, are the most disadvantaged of all our citizens, in terms of substandard housing, extremely high rates of unemployment and very low incomes. It is no coincidence that, as a group, they are also have the poorest overall health status of all Canadians, with a life expectancy seven years less than that of the overall population and a rate of infant mortality almost twice that of the overall population.

We have seen that poor housing is associated with poor health and that level of income generally determines the type of housing people have. Increasing numbers of Canadians without income have no housing at all, with disastrous consequences for their health. And, while unemployment may affect health because it causes stress and loss of social support networks, much of that stress arises through the loss of income that goes with the loss of a job.

Poverty may result from unemployment, especially when social programs to replace income for the unemployed are cut back. Hundreds of studies in many different countries, both in the developed and less-developed world, have demonstrated the impact of poverty on health. Not to put too fine a point on it — poverty kills.

There is really no consensus about how many people are poor in Canada. While Statistics Canada collects data on low incomes, it defines "low income" in relative terms. Its "Low-Income Cut-Offs" (LICOs) are based on the percentage of income that individuals and families spend on the basic needs of food, clothing and shelter, in comparison with the rest of the population. Based on the Family Expenditure Survey of 1992, the average family spends about 37.4% of its pre-tax income on these basic needs.

To calculate the LICO, Statistics Canada assumes that any family spending 20 percentage points more than the average family on basic needs would be in "straitened circumstances." In other words, families falling below the LICOs generally spend 57.4% or more of their pre-tax income on food, clothing and shelter. Statistics Canada also publishes LICOs based on the pattern of spending indicated by the 1986 Family Expenditure Survey, and it calculates other low-income statistics referred to as Low Income Measures (LIMs). It also calculates low-income data on an after-tax basis. But the pre-tax LICO is the measure of low-income that most people use to assess poverty.

Statistics Canada is careful to point out that, although its low-income-cut-offs are commonly referred to as poverty lines, "they have no officially recognized status, nor does Statistics Canada promote their use as poverty lines."[84] However, the National Council of Welfare, which regularly constructs a comprehensive *Poverty Profile* of the Canadian population, takes the position that, "Regardless of the terminology, the cut-offs are a useful tool for defining and analyzing the significantly large portion of the Canadian population with low incomes. They are not the only measures of poverty used in Canada, but

they are the most widely accepted and are roughly comparable to most alternative measures."[85]

Recent trends in poverty rates in Canada

According to the LICOs based on 1992 family expenditures,
the incidence of low income among all Canadians declined from
a peak of 18.8% in 1984 to a low of 14.1% in 1989. By 1993, as a
result of the recession of 1991-1992, the rate had risen again to
18.0%. It dropped to 17.1% in 1994, but has increased since then
to reach 17.9% in 1996.[86]

There are significant differences in rates of low income
between different family types and between women and men.
The table on the next page shows a selection of low-income

Incidence of low income for selected family types Estimates based on Low Income Cut-Offs, 1992 base (percentage of those in each category with incomes below the cut-off) Canada

Year	Children under age 18	Elderly aged 65 and over	Two-parent families with children	Female lone-parent families	Unattached elderly women
1986	17.6	26.6	10.9	57.7	61.2
1987	17.7	25.4	10.3	58.3	59.3
1988	16.1	25.8	9.1	55.3	61.4
1989	15.3	22.4	8.7	52.9	56.6
1990	17.8	21.3	9.8	59.5	53.8
1991	18.9	21.9	10.8	60.3	54.2
1992	19.2	20.8	10.6	56.9	54.0
1993	21.3	22.8	12.2	59.0	56.4
1994	19.5	19.3	11.5	56.4	52.9
1995	21.0	18.7	12.8	56.8	50.6
1996	21.1	20.8	11.8	60.8	53.4

*Source: Statistics Canada Income Distributions by Size in Canada - 1996.
Catalogue 13-207-XPB. Text Tables III and IV.*

rates for different family types and individuals over an 11-year period, from 1986 to 1996.

It is striking that low-income rates are extremely high for some groups within the Canadian population. Almost 61% of lone-parent families headed by women have incomes below the LICOs. In fact, Statistics Canada estimated that, on average, low-income families in this category had incomes that were more than $9,000 below the cut-offs. This measure gauges the depth of poverty and is referred to as the "average income deficiency."

While low-income rates for elderly unattached women were also very high, it was estimated that the average income deficiency for low-income women in this group was about $3,300, no doubt thanks to public pension programs which account for 65% of the income of women aged 65 and older.[87] As some observers have noted, social programs that provide income have reduced the number of poor seniors in Canada. But many have been lifted just barely above the poverty level by the various income programs. Instead of being poor, they are now simply "near poor."[88] In the case of elderly women on their own, they are still poor, but not quite as poor as they used to be.

Given the acknowledged links between poverty and health, it must surely be of concern to policy-makers that low-income rates for the most disadvantaged groups have been rising for the past three years. In relation to the socioeconomic factors that are so important to population health, there are some disturbing trends behind the numbers. It would appear that continuing high unemployment and cuts to government social programs are largely responsible for increased rates of low income in Canada.

Statistics Canada says that a number of factors contributed to the change in the level and distribution of family income in 1996. Because about 80% of family income comes from earnings, the performance of the labour market remains key. And labour market performance in 1996 was "lackluster." Employment grew by only 1.3% in 1996 and only half the gains in employment were full-time jobs. The trend to self-employment may also have been a factor, according to Statistics Canada, since self-employed persons tend to earn less, on average, than paid workers.[89] In fact, labour force survey data show that growth in self-employment has more than doubled since the mid-1970s, far outpacing growth in the number of paid employees. More than three-quarters of the job growth since 1989 has been in self-employment.[90]

But Statistics Canada also noted that, for lower-income families, transfer payments are just as important as earnings, since a greater proportion of the income of these families has traditionally come from this source. And government transfer payments to families continued to decline in 1996. Employment Insurance payments were down again, as were social assistance payments. As a result, said Statistics Canada, 1996 was the third straight year that the proportion of family income from transfers decreased.[91]

Income distribution and population health

It is evident that many of the socioeconomic determinants of population health are closely inter-connected. Unemployment can result in poverty; poverty may determine the type of housing a family has; educational levels may limit the earnings of individuals; early childhood development may limit a person's educational opportunities. All of these elements may explain why some individuals are healthy and others are not. But they do not explain why the population of some countries appears to be healthier than the population of others.

Research on health inequalities within developed countries has increasingly focused on the relationship of the individual to society: on how people are affected by social position; by wealth and poverty; by job insecurity and unemployment; by education; by social mobility; on the importance of social networks; on family disruption; on stress at work and the social organization of work.[92] Wilkinson says that, instead of looking to see what makes one individual healthier than another, his aim in *Unhealthy Societies: the Afflictions of Inequality* was to see what makes one society healthier than any other. He notes that, "From the points of view of practical politics and public policy, or indeed of its sociological interest, it is the health of whole societies which matters."[93] The overriding issue, he says, is how to increase the sum total of health enjoyed by society.

No one doubts the importance of living standards to health when we compare one country with another, he says. But why is life expectancy higher in countries like Greece, Japan, Iceland and Italy than it is in richer countries like the United States or Germany?[94] In the developed world, he says, it is not the richest countries which have the best health, but the most egalitarian. The quality of the social life of a society is one of the most powerful determinants of health. And this, in turn, is very closely related to the degree of income inequality, he notes.

Within countries, the differences in the standard of living establish a social ordering of the population. What affects health, he says, is no longer the differences in absolute material standards, but social position within societies. Countries in which the income differences between rich and poor are larger (meaning more or deeper relative poverty) tend to have worse health than countries in which the differences are smaller. Life expectancy in countries like Sweden and Norway, where the poorest 70% of households received a larger share of income than elsewhere, is higher than it is in countries like the former West Germany and the United States, which were less egalitarian.

Looking at the period from 1975 to 1985, for example, research shows that those countries of the European Union that reduced the proportion of their population living in relative poverty — for example, France and Greece — enjoyed faster increases in life expectancy than those in which relative poverty increased.

Wilkinson also notes that the relationship between income distribution and life expectancy was first discovered in data from both rich and poor countries. Statistically significant relationships have now been reported by at least eight different research groups using some ten separate sets of data drawn at different dates, from different groups of developed and developing countries on cross-sectional and time series bases.[95]

According to Wilkinson, the evidence of a relationship between economic equality and population mortality rates is much too strong to be dismissed, and it is found on too many different bases for it to be an expression of some intervening variable. But he points out there may still be questions about which came first: does income distribution affect health, for example, or does poor health somehow determine income distribution? To suggest that health somehow influences income distribution, he says, runs counter to economic theory and flies in the face of common-sense notions of the influence on income distribution of employment and unemployment, profits, taxes and benefits. Research has looked at the possibility that health inequalities appear because people with good health move up the social scale, while those with poor health move down. While this does happen to some extent, it does not account for the bulk of health inequalities.

Wilkinson concludes that "It is now clear that the scale of income differences in a society is one of the most powerful determinants of health standards in different countries, and that it influences health through its impact on social cohesion."[96] He also suggests that, while researchers have grown used to thinking about the determinants of individual health, they have given little attention to the broader questions which policy-makers need answered. Yet the explanations of what makes whole populations healthier than others may be very different from the evidence which comes out of studies of what makes some individuals healthier than others.

If health inequalities were due to poverty, he asks, why have they gotten bigger in countries such as Britain during the last 50 years, despite huge rises in the standard of living? According to Wilkinson, the evidence suggests that what matters within societies is not so much the direct health effects of absolute material living standards so much as the effects of social relatives. The crucial evidence, he says, comes from the discovery of a strong international relationship between income distribution and national mortality rates.

Data from the landmark Inquiry into Income and Wealth by the Joseph Rowntree Foundation in the U.K. seem to prove the point — particularly in relation to the past two decades in Britain.[97] This report found that inequality in incomes in Britain started to rise after 1978-79. The most striking feature, says this report, is the rise of the share of the richest one-fifth. By 1993, their share of (equivalized) disposable income was 42%, compared with 35% in 1978. Meanwhile, the share of the poorest one-fifth had fallen from 9.8% to 7.6% (up from a minimum of 7.0% in 1990). The bulk of this fall occurred in the second half of the 1980s.[98]

Author Will Hutton, in his 1995 book *The State We're In,*[99] notes that the British experience of "radical marketization" under Margaret Thatcher offers a "salutary warning to others." The growth of inequality, he says, "has been the fastest of any advanced state." The Rowntree Report notes that, in fact, inequality was increasing even faster in New Zealand during the 1980s. (It is perhaps of interest to note that New Zealand also went through a radical restructuring and "marketization" after the 1984 election, which included massive privatization of the public sector, deregulation, major cutbacks in social programs, and the introduction of a GST). But in most other countries where inequality was increasing, it was doing so at less than half the British rate.[100]

Writing in 1996, Wilkinson says the effects of widening income differences on local disparities and on the rate of reduction in national mortality rates were already evident. Most of the growth in income inequality in Britain during the 1980s took place among people of working age and their children. Relative poverty among old people increased only very slightly during this period. But it is among the younger age groups that the mortality impact of the widening income differences is to be found.

Wilkinson looked at infant mortality and mortality rates of children aged 1-19 and adults aged 20-44. He found that from 1985 onwards, the rate of mortality decline slowed down in each age group. Is it mere coincidence that rapidly widening income differentials were accompanied by a marked slowing down of improvement in mortality rates? Wilkinson says there is strong evidence from three separate studies that the two are causally related. All three studies found that socioeconomic differences between electoral wards had widened during the decade (from 1981 to 1991) and that this was matched by a widening differential in death rates.[101]

As deprivation in some areas increased, mortality in some age groups in the poorest areas actually rose. In other age

groups, they simply failed to fall. It is likely that similar processes affected mortality in the United States. As income differences widened there during the 1980s, the rate at which the
population's life expectancy improved also slowed down. The
national slow-down was associated particularly with a decline
in life expectancy among the black population.

Wilkinson points out that, although we do not know
whether more advantaged groups also saw a slow-down in the
decline of their mortality rates (American whites include poor
whites), we do know, he says, that their increasing relative
incomes do not cause a compensating acceleration in the decline in their death rates that would counterbalance the damage done to the less well-off. If relative income makes a difference to health, then, as an abstract idea, says Wilkinson, one
might be surprised if increases in the relative incomes of those
already at the top of the heap do not lead to more rapid improvements in their health. However, thinking about this in
any practical context, he says, "there is no reason why the
health of the rich should gain as a result of increasing social
tensions, despair and degeneration in the inner city areas."[102]
No one suggests that the health of the rich might in any way
benefit from the fact that death rates in Harlem are at most
ages higher than in rural Bangladesh.

Looking at a number of different examples of healthy egalitarian societies, Wilkinson says an important characteristic
they all seem to share is their social cohesion. They have a
strong community life. The individualism and the values of the
market are restrained by a social morality, and these societies
have more of what has been called "social capital" which lubri-
cates the workings of the whole society and economy. There
are few signs of anti-social aggressiveness, and society appears
to be more caring.[103]

Health is telling us a story about the major influences on the quality of life in modern societies, says Wilkinson, and it is a story we cannot afford to ignore. It addresses the increasing disquiet about the contrast between the material success and the social failure of modern societies. The extent to which the quality of life has been equated with the material standard of living is remarkable, says Wilkinson. This is no doubt because of the difficulty of measuring the social quality of life.

In fact, researchers in Canada have attempted to measure the quality of social health, and their findings appear to support the implication of Wilkinson's comment that a material standard of living is not necessarily a good indication of population health. The Index of Social Health (ISH), constructed by Satya Brink and Allen Zeesman of Human Resources Development Canada, uses a set of socioeconomic indicators covering 15 social issues dealing with health, mortality, poverty, unemployment, inequality, and access to services.[104] The ISH is modelled on the well-known Fordham Index of Social Health developed by Marc Miringhof at the Institute for Innovation in Social Policy at Fordham University in New York State.

Brink and Zeesman plotted the ISH against Gross Domestic Product per capita at 1996 prices for the years from 1970 to 1995. They found that the growth in the ISH closely matched the increase in GDP throughout the 1970s. Continuous increases in real average weekly earnings and the related declines in the poverty rates of children and the elderly contributed to the increase in the Index during this period. But, while GDP per capita continued to climb right through the period to 1995, the ISH declined sharply between 1980 and 1983. It remained relatively stable until 1989, after which it showed two years of decline. After a brief recovery, the Index flattened out at the level experienced in the 1970s.

Brink and Zeesman say that declines in the Index in the early 1980s and 1990s appear to be linked to the recessions experienced in those time periods. Declines may be attributed to higher rates of unemployment, falling real wages, and increases in child poverty. But the key point to note, these authors say, is that a recovery in the GDP is not reflected in the ISH because unemployment continued to be high and real wages continued to slide.

Brink and Zeesman say that, in comparison with the United States, Canada has lost the ground it gained in the seventies, falling to its approximate starting point. The United States, on the other hand, compared to its own performance, continuously declined during the entire period. "This raises the question," they say, "whether the social programs in Canada supported the growth in the 1970s, and whether they have had a moderating effect, as the two countries have very similar contexts, except for these programs."[105]

Index of Social Health and GDP (1986 Prices), Canada 1970-1995

Source: Satya Brink and Allen Zeesman, **Measuring Social Well-Being: An Index of Social Health for Canada.** Applied Research Branch, Strategic Policy, Human Resources Development Canada. June 1997.

It is also interesting to observe that data presented in the 1998 federal budget indicate that total program spending as a percentage of GDP is now lower than it was in the 1970s. Finance Minister Paul Martin announced further reductions to bring program spending down to the level of the late 1940s, so that, by the 1999-2000 fiscal year, total program spending as a percentage of GDP will be at its lowest level in 50 years.[106]

Social cohesion

In considering the issue of social cohesion, Wilkinson reviewed a number of studies, including studies of Japan, which simultaneously achieved an unusually narrow income distribution and the highest life expectancy in the world, and of wartime Britain. He notes that the most rapid improvements in life expectancy in Britain during the 20th century came during the two world wars. In the decades which include the two world wars, life expectancy increased by between six and seven years for both men and women. This is well over twice as fast as the average rate of improvement during the rest of the cen-

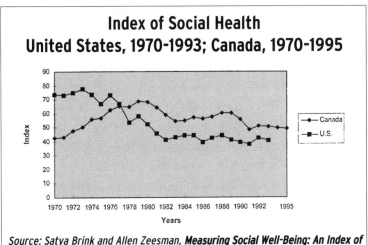

Index of Social Health
United States, 1970-1993; Canada, 1970-1995

*Source: Satya Brink and Allen Zeesman, **Measuring Social Well-Being: An Index of Social Health for Canada**. Applied Research Branch, Strategic Policy, Human Resources Development Canada. June 1997.*

tury.[107] Life during the war, he says, is always described in terms of the sense of camaraderie, or of people pulling together, and a sense of social cohesion. Even though absolute material standards deteriorated for much of the population during wartime, both wars saw a return to full employment and a dramatic narrowing of income differences. The reduction of unemployment removed a source of social division and bitterness, while at the same time giving people a role in a common task, Wilkinson says.

Studies of Roseto, a small town in Pennsylvania; of certain regions in Italy; of Eastern Europe during the 1970s and 1980s; and of Japan — all illustrated in various ways how narrowed income differentials promote social cohesion and improved population health. The message that comes through clearly in each case, says Wilkinson, is that the healthy, egalitarian countries have — or had — a sense of social cohesion and public-spiritedness. "Social rather than market values remained dominant in the public sphere of life."[108] That social cohesion is very strongly related to income distribution, he says, "is a message no politician should be allowed to ignore."[109]

Income distribution in Canada

The 1996 ACPH *Report on the Health of Canadians* acknowledged that income distribution is very important to population health. "The more equal the distribution of wealth, the healthier the population," said the report. Data on income inequality show that there has been a tendency towards growing inequality in terms of earned income in Canada.[110]

In fact, Statistics Canada reported that, although overall average family income was little changed in 1996, the gap between rich and poor widened. Lower earnings and lower transfer payments resulted in an average loss of income of 3% or $500 for the one-fifth of families with the lowest incomes. Families in this income group depend heavily on transfers — including Child Tax Benefit, Old Age Security, Employment Insurance and Social Assistance — which provided 59% of their income in 1996.

The one-fifth of families with the highest incomes saw their incomes rise by 1.8%, or $2,000 on average, in 1996. For these families, Statistics Canada said, substantial improvements in earnings more than offset reduced returns from investments. In 1995, these were the only families to realize income gains.

Recent studies pinpoint unemployment as a key factor in increasing inequality of family market incomes in Canada. (Family market income is income from all sources other than government transfer payments). A joint study by Andrew Sharpe of the Centre for the Study of Living Standards and analyst Myles Zyblock reviewed the period from 1975 to 1994 and found that the secular rise in the unemployment rate in Canada accounted for about one-third of the increase in family market income inequality over the past 20 years. The key policy implication, these authors say, is that, "While by no means a panacea, lower unemployment is a necessary condition for a return to an era of less disparity in market income."[111]

The Caledon Institute also notes that there has been a marked increase in inequality of market income since 1980. Minimum wages are too low to support a family, and are not indexed. Between 1995 and 1996, Caledon says, the value of minimum wages fell in some provinces, remained the same in others, and increased somewhat in other provinces. Overall, though, the average of all provincial minimum wages declined from $5.69 an hour in 1995 to $5.44 an hour in 1996.[112] Recent cuts to social programs, in particular unemployment insurance and welfare, have hurt poor and modest-income Canadians, Caledon says. In 1996, average transfer payments to families in the lowest income quintile fell by 3%. As a result, the average total income of families in the bottom group declined by 3% between 1995 and 1996.

Unemployment Insurance (now known as Employment Insurance) has been tightened significantly, Caledon notes, resulting in a dramatic reduction in the percentage of the unemployed qualifying for benefits, lower average payments, and a shorter maximum duration of benefits. The percentage of unemployed Canadians receiving unemployment benefits plunged from 86.8% in 1990 to 48.1% in 1996.[113] Caledon also notes that welfare benefits have declined in all provinces — dramatically so in Ontario. But it says that welfare cuts are not a major cause of rising poverty because welfare benefits in all provinces were far below the poverty line even before recent reductions in some provinces.

Statistics Canada explains that transfers and income taxes have the effect of lowering inequality within any given year. Historically, inequality measured on income before transfers has grown more than inequality calculated using total income, while after-tax income inequality (inequality measured on income after payment of income taxes) has remained stable.

During the period from 1980 to 1995, the data show the dampening and equalizing effects of transfers and taxes on income swings through periods of recession and growth. Statistics Canada reported that, since 1980, economic downturns saw the income gap grow significantly between high- and low-income families before transfers and taxes. During the recovery of the 1980s, this gap was reduced. However, the improvement was not enough to counter the inequality increases associated with the 1981-82 recession. The recession of the early 1990s saw another increase in inequality. The result over this 15-year period, Statistics Canada says, was a trend to increased pre-transfer, pre-tax income inequality. But, after transfers and taxes, there was virtually no increase.[114]

Since 1994, the agency reported, before-tax inequality has edged upwards. Whether or not the long-standing trend in after-tax income inequality also has been affected cannot be determined until after-tax family income estimates are compiled in the spring of 1998, Statistics Canada says.[115]

The *Report on the Health of Canadians* notes that while, in terms of earned income (before taxes and transfers), the gap between rich and poor is growing, "So far, the social safety net — through income tax, unemployment insurance, social assistance, and other transfer programs — has been able to offset the trend toward inequality in earnings." But this report concedes that "It is possible that the social safety net will not be able to continue to compensate for these growing inequalities. This may result in worse quality of life for the population."[116]

In its 1997 paper on *Health Impacts of Social and Economic Conditions: Implications for Public Policy,* the CPHA observed that "social programs are far more effective than most people realize in combatting the growing inequality that threatens Canada's economic health and social stability." Social programs and a progressive tax system have helped to reduce dramatically the gap in market incomes between high-income and low-income Canadians. But substantial cuts to certain programs in recent years, says the CPHA, "raise serious questions as to their continued ability to reduce the growing gaps in market income."[117]

The gaps in research

We now have a wide range of research and knowledge about the socioeconomic determinants of population health. In Canada, recent trends in many of these variables raise cause for concern. There appears to have been little effort at the level of national public policy to monitor these trends in relation to their impact on the overall health of the Canadian population. We still do not seem to have made a concerted effort — at least at the level of national public policy — to "help identify health risks related to adverse economic conditions," as the WHO urged countries to do, nor to answer the questions on socioeconomic trends posed by the WHO.

How has overall population health been affected by trends in employment and unemployment, and are there identifiable groups which have become or are becoming disenfranchised? Are government revenues sufficient to sustain an adequate level of public expenditure? And what has been the impact on population health of recent cutbacks in government spending at all levels — federal, provincial and municipal? How is the country's wealth spread throughout the population? We know that inequality has increased over the past two decades, but can we determine how increasing inequality has affected population health? Are existing social programs adequate to protect disadvantaged groups within our society and to ensure their health? What impact will recent cuts in those programs have on income inequalities and ultimately on the health of our population?

Are the economic prospects expected to improve the present distribution of income? If structural adjustment policies have been necessary, what has been their impact? Have the effects of unemployment had an influence on income distribution — some of the studies referred to earlier indicate that there has been a negative impact — and, if so, is this situation changing, and how? Are significant sectors of the society excluded, because of age, sex, education, race, ethnic identity, or for other reasons, from full participation in the life of the society, including equitable access to employment, social protection, education, and life-chances? (We have considerable evidence that young people, Aboriginal people and women —

particularly those who are lone-parent heads of families and those who are elderly and alone — are indeed excluded.) To what extent is this situation affecting health status within the country as a whole, and for the specific groups? How have all these developments had an impact on the health of the Canadian population?

Other areas for further research have been identified throughout this Chapter. Most notable among them is the need for a gender analysis of the socioeconomic factors that affect the health of populations. Studies based on males only, as a great many of the studies in this field appear to be, cannot be generalized as applicable to the entire population, as they have been in many cases. Gender-sensitive research and analysis is needed, not just to identify health differences between women and men as individuals, but to determine how women's different lifetime experiences — and in particular the way in which they must combine paid and unpaid work — are having an impact on the overall health of the Canadian population.

As we expand our knowledge in this area, the challenge will be to develop and implement social and economic policies that will help to reduce health inequalities in Canada and improve the overall health of our population.

Chapter 3
THE POLICY CHALLENGE

In spite of the need for further research in certain areas, as identified in the last Chapter, there is plenty of evidence that socioeconomic trends have a major impact on the health of our population. And there is also reason to think that population health has been affected by recent socioeconomic trends in Canada. There is little doubt that the quality of life in Canada has been deteriorating for the greater part of the past 20 years. The Applied Research Branch of Human Resources Development Canada says that trends now point to the risk of a growing underclass among disadvantaged Canadians. This is just one of five significant and unsettling challenges identified in a 1995 social outlook prepared by the Branch.[1]

Canadians now face five crucial challenges, according to this document:

- **Under investment in human capital.** Much of Canada's labour force — its human capital — is inadequately prepared for today's economic reality. Too often, education and training systems in Canada are failing to adjust to the increasing demands of the new information economy.
- **The wasted productivity of 1.4 million unemployed Canadians.** Globalization and technological change are altering industrial structures, but many individuals can't keep up with the changes. When workers do not have appropriate skills, the result is unemployment. Some major barriers

for the unemployed — at least according to HRDC's social outlook — are low levels of education combined with a lack of access to learning opportunities, a lack of jobs in certain regions, and low levels of public spending on active programming to get people back to work.

- **Growing economic insecurity among the middle class.** The middle class is stressed out and insecure, says this document. Real earnings for full-time, full-year earners have stagnated since the mid-1970s. Older workers (45+) are experiencing increasingly long spells of unemployment — up from 17 weeks in 1976 to 32 weeks in 1993. (More recent data for 1996 show little improvement, with average duration of unemployment for workers aged 45+ at 31.3 weeks.[2]) Those who find re-employment often suffer a decline in their wage rate.

- **The potential for a lost generation of youth.** Even though they are much better educated than previous generations, today's full-time, full-year young workers have significantly lower real earnings than their counterparts in the mid-1970s (22.6% less for young men, 3.4% less for young women). Combine this with the increasing difficulty of finding stable employment, and the result is increased poverty for all types of young families.

Indicators of social health

The standard of living of societies has traditionally been measured by their GDP per capita. Over recent years, however, there has been strong pressure for the development of social indicators, or indicators of well-being — mainly because the traditional economic indicators do not seem to reflect accurately what many people feel is the reality of their lives. Such indicators often contain a number of socioeconomic variables and may therefore serve as a rough guide to likely recent trends in overall population health.

The Index of Social Health (ISH), constructed by Satya Brink and Allen Zeesman at Human Resources Development Canada and referred to earlier, plots quite dramatically what has been going on. It shows that, while Canada's GDP per capita has been steadily increasing over the past 25 years, the social health of the Canadian population has been declining since about 1980. Of particular interest is that, while GDP per capita had dropped in the early 1990s, it recovered in the three years from 1993 to 1995. But in that same three-year period, the ISH was declining.

As noted earlier, 15 social indicators were used to construct the Index of Social Health. Many are known to have an impact on overall population health as it is generally defined. Some variables, such as infant mortality, are actually generally accepted health measures. It may therefore be assumed that the ISH is a reasonable guide to the direction of some of the key socioeconomic elements that are so crucial to the health of

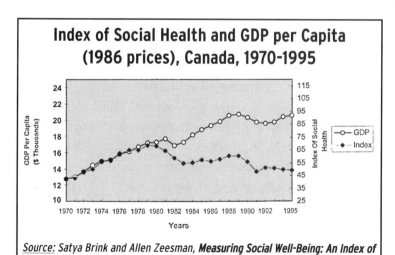

Index of Social Health and GDP per Capita (1986 prices), Canada, 1970-1995

Source: Satya Brink and Allen Zeesman, *Measuring Social Well-Being: An Index of Social Health for Canada. Applied Research Branch, Strategic Policy, Human Resources Development Canada. June 1997.*

Canada's population. The definitions used in the construction of the Index are as follows:

- **Infant mortality** — using the infant mortality rate, or the number of deaths of children less than one year of age per thousand live births.
- **Child abuse** — the number of children injured as a result of assault, abuse, battering, or neglect.
- **Child poverty** — based on the number of children under 18 living under the Low Income Cut-Off (LICO).
- **Teen suicide** — suicide rates for ages 15 to 19 years per 100,000 population.
- **Drug abuse** — based on the number of juvenile offenders (charged and not charged) involved in federal drug offences, including consumption of cannabis, cocaine, heroin and other drugs, controlled drugs and restricted drugs covered under the federal Food and Drugs Act.
- **High school drop-outs** — the drop-out rate for secondary school students (Grade 9 and up).
- **Unemployment** — using the unemployment rate for Canada and the provinces.
- **Average weekly earnings** — for all employees, with data adjusted to 1986 dollars.
- **Poverty among those aged 65 and over** — that is, the number of persons 65 and over below the LICOs.
- **Out-of-pocket health expenditures for persons 65 and over** — based on the percentage of income spent on health care expenses by persons 65 years and over.
- **Highway deaths related to alcohol** — fatally injured drivers, 16 years and over, where the blood alcohol contents (BAC in mg%) exceeded 80.
- **Homicides** — per 100,000 population.

- **Persons receiving social assistance** — the number of beneficiaries of the Canada Assistance Plan. (The ISH was plotted for the period up to 1995. CAP was abolished by the federal government, effective from the fiscal year 1996/97 onwards, when it was replaced with the Canada Health and Social Transfer).
- **Gap between rich and poor** — using the difference between percentage distribution of aggregate income received by the top and bottom quintiles.
- **Access to affordable housing** — based on the proportion of income spent on carrying costs (principal, interest and taxes) for first-time home buyers.

Could social indicators be used as a guide for policy-makers? Many observers raise serious concerns about the possibility. There is considerable pressure for a simple guide to socioeconomic trends that policies need to address. But there are also real dangers in simplifying complex relationships between various socioeconomic developments and trying to express them in terms of one overall index number.

Mike McCracken and Katherine Scott, in a 1998 paper on *Social and Economic Indicators,*[3] warn that the predominant model of social and economic indicators rests on a few fundamental assumptions about what constitutes knowledge and its production. Inherent in the indicator project, they emphasize, is the idea that one can reduce complex social and economic phenomena (empirical reality) to a single meaningful statement or stylized fact, that there is a direct correspondence between an indicator such as the unemployment rate and an experience, event or condition.

Indeed, the value of indicators for policy-making, say these authors, resides in precisely the fact that they are ostensibly grounded in empirical reality and not in knowledge derived from theory, intuition, or deduction. Indicators and other empirical tools are held up as **value-free** science, say McCracken and Scott, and of course they are nothing of the sort. Indicators are not neutral statistical concepts. They validate particular world views and prioritize select areas of knowledge. The patina of objectivity is compounded if and when indicators are institutionalized, say these authors. Usage over time tends to reify a particular understanding and measurement of an issue such as unemployment or productivity, making it into an objective reality rather than a social construction that privileges established interests and world views — in government, in business, or in academe.[4]

As well, these authors point out, the reasons why policy-makers are so interested in indicators have changed. They explain that, while work on social indicators dates back to the 19th century, the social indicator movement really gained impetus in the 1960s and early 1970s when questions were being raised about just what "progress" really meant.[5] The Economic Council of Canada undertook to explore social indicators to broaden the discussion of goals, and proposed a set of indicators for health, housing and the environment, as well as encouraging the development of underlying databases. The development of social indicators was seen as a key to crafting a more activist social policy, and the measurement of change was seen as an important part of the government's role in society.

But McCracken and Scott note that, as the development of welfare states in the 1960s marshalled interest in social indicators, perhaps not surprisingly there has been a resurgence of interest in social indicators in the 1990s as governments dismantle welfare programs. The sources of interest in the 1990s are much different. They identify three key driving forces behind the current pressure to develop social indicators:

- **Decision-makers are currently embracing "evidence-based" decision-making in an effort to redefine the role of the modern state.** There is a new focus on "outcome" measures within government to understand how well existing policies and programs are meeting their stated objectives, and to determine what activities government should be pursuing in the future. In many cases, decision-makers do not have the information necessary to assess the success or failure of programs — particularly programs which attempt to achieve social goals such as greater equality — and are consequently sponsoring research into indicator development. (Health Canada, for example, is now developing indicators of population health. And in November 1996, the Canadian Council on Social Development held a major symposium on social indicators under the title of *Measuring Well-being*,[6] with participants from across Canada, along with several from the United States and Europe.)

- **The relationship between the citizen and the state is changing.** At a time when the public is increasingly skeptical about governments, many citizen groups are demanding greater accountability from their public officials. These demands take many forms, ranging from public accounting (or value for money) to greater popular participation in setting the goals and limits of state activity (for example, laws on public referendums). The well-known Oregon Benchmarks project[7] is a good example of renewed interest in social indicators within government and by the general public. This project was created with extensive public input to set out long-term social and economic goals for the state of Oregon and to chart progress toward these goals.

Benchmarks were adopted by the last two sessions of the Oregon state legislature, and they are used as the basis for building the state budget. Various communities throughout the state have also adopted locally-oriented benchmarks systems. According to Oregon's Internet Web site,[8] the benchmarks "form a collective effort by state and local governments, civic groups, non-profits and businesses to appreciably improve the lives of Oregonians and self-regulated individuals, members of healthy families, and skilled, successful workers." There are 272 benchmarks in total, dealing with a range of social and economic issues, from teen pregnancy rates and infant mortality to literacy and environmental standards.

- **The voluntary sector and various advocacy movements in Canada have also embraced social indicators as a means of monitoring progress as governments at the federal and provincial level restructure welfare state programs.** Progressive social groups point out that governments have conquered their deficits at the expense of low- and middle-income Canadians. They are using social indicators to make their case that investing in programs like the Child Tax Benefit or child care makes good economic sense, both in the short-term (lower rates/depth of child poverty) and in the long term (improved well-being and productivity of all citizens).

The criticism of social indicators, of course, is based on the fact that they reflect the values of those who design them. As McCracken and Scott explain, while most people would agree that an indicator is "a set of rules for gathering and organizing data so they can be assigned meaning,"[9] every indicator starts with some view of how the world works, or should work. This is reflected in the data used, the weighting, the time frame

Health and Wealth

analyzed, and choices about method and disaggregation (regional, gender, age, etc.). An indicator highlights certain aspects of a situation at the expense of others, allowing observers to "see" the world through a particular lens, channeling thoughts and actions in particular directions.[10]

Many social indicators — including the ISH developed by Brink and Zeesman — ignore gender differences, for example. They may then present a misleading picture of socioeconomic trends because they do not reflect inequalities between women and men. The United Nations Human Development Index (HDI), which we have been told many times shows that Canada is "the best place in the world to live," compares countries on three basic measures only: life expectancy, educational attainment, and per capita income. But the annual report on the HDI also includes a gender development index which adjusts the HDI for inequality between women and men. It turns out that, when women's experience is factored in, Canada is no longer at the top of the list. The question to be asked here, of course, is whether an indicator that fails to include gender equality measures can be considered adequate or credible as a measure of the "human development" of any society.

GDP per capita excludes much of the work that women do, because it is unpaid. In fact, much of the work related to measurement of well-being overlooks differences between women and men and is insensitive to gender issues. An interdepartmental committee, incorporating a number of federal government departments, has recently been wrestling with the issue of social cohesion. It has defined "social cohesion" as "an ongoing process of developing a community of shared values, shared challenges and equal opportunity in Canada." Of course, people who have worked with equality-seeking groups would recognize immediately that providing "equal opportunity" for disadvantaged people who have suffered generations of inequality does not move us very far towards equality or justice, which presumably is what we need if we are to achieve "social cohesion." And what about "shared values"? Do those shared values include values of gender equality? We don't know.[11]

The need for action

Regardless of what indicators are used to monitor socio-economic trends and to provide warning signals to policy-makers who are concerned about the health of the population, there is no avoiding the fact that we already have plenty of evidence of the socioeconomic basis for health inequalities — but so far, very little action to address them. If policy-makers are really serious about improving population health, then the socioeconomic issues will have to be addressed. In terms of the Population Health pyramid which we show here, Canada has a strong foundation, in that it has recognized the socioeconomic determinants of population health. But it has not moved very far up through the next four levels to reach the goal of population health. And it certainly has not gone very far towards meeting the WHO goal of health for all by the year 2000.

Building Toward Population Health

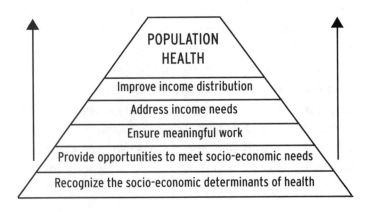

POPULATION
HEALTH

Improve income distribution

Address income needs

Ensure meaningful work

Provide opportunities to meet socio-economic needs

Recognize the socio-economic determinants of health

Health and Wealth

There is no doubt that serious efforts to address the socio-economic factors that determine population health present a major challenge. Canada has taken tiny steps along the road — for example, in limited efforts to address child poverty, literacy, and educational opportunities. But such efforts pale beside the magnitude of the problems. Considerable political determination would be needed to deal with major areas such as unemployment, housing, adult poverty, and early childhood development. Most challenging of all is the question of income distribution, especially in light of the growing gap between rich and poor in Canada.

Are economic prospects expected to improve the present distribution of income? Are government revenues sufficient to sustain an adequate level of public expenditure? Those were both questions the World Health Organization suggested countries ask themselves in developing strategies to achieve health for all by the year 2000. In terms of public policy on population health, Canada has not yet answered them. So far, the tax/transfer system has been able largely to offset the growing inequalities between rich and poor. But for how long?

Canadians have been told that, over the next couple of years, program spending by the federal government is to be reduced to its lowest level in 50 years when measured as a percentage of GDP.[12] Fifty years ago, Canada had only minimal public pensions and it did not have Medicare or unemployment insurance. A return to the spending levels of the 1940s must therefore be cause for serious concern. Sharply reduced program spending at the federal level has been accompanied by severe cutbacks in spending at provincial levels, too, as transfers from the federal government to the provinces have also been cut. In its 1996 *Report on the Health of Canadians,* the Advisory Committee on Population Health warned of the possibility that the social safety net will not be able to continue to compensate for growing inequalities. The result would be a worse quality of life for the population — and almost certainly a decline in population health.[13]

In terms of the socioeconomic influences on population health, the ACPH report highlighted several trends that give rise to concern because of their potential impact on the health of Canadians:

- Unemployment is affecting a large number of Canadians, and those numbers remain high.
- Child poverty rates in Canada, particularly for children in single-parent families, are very high compared to rates in other industrialized countries, and are showing no sign of improvement. (In fact, since this report was written, based on 1994 data, the number of children being raised in poor families has increased even further).
- Inequalities in earned income are growing and could well lead to a growing number of the poor, if the social safety net becomes inadequate to counterbalance the trend.[14]

The political will to act

Whether or not Canada has the political will to tackle such problems in the name of population health — or even simply in the name of social justice — remains to be seen. To repeat: there has been ample documentation of the adverse effets that socioeconomic factors have on the health of individuals, as well as on the overall health of the population. There is evidence that policy-makers are well aware of this reality. But actually addressing the fundamental basis of health inequalities is another matter.

The experience of the Working Group on Inequalities in Health in Britain is instructive. Its mandate was to assemble available information about the differences in health status among the social classes and about factors which might contribute to these, including relevant data from other industrial countries; to analyze this material so as to identify possible causal relationships; to examine the hypotheses that have been formulated and the testing of them; to assess the implications for policy; and to suggest what further research might be needed.[15] Its 1980 report — the Black Report — was released after three years of study and was followed by another report seven years later, *The Health Divide: Inequalities in Health in the 1980s,* published by the Health Education Council before it was disbanded by the Thatcher government in 1987.

Both reports received a very hostile reception from the Conservative government of the day. But the health professions and the research community took the findings of the two reports seriously. There was widespread agreement on the three main premises in the reports: 1) that in absolute terms the standards of health of the population as a whole had improved since the Second World War; 2) that, despite thais improvement, serious social inequalities in health had persisted; and 3) that socioeconomic factors had played an important part in maintaining and even increasing these differentials.[16]

In an introduction to a 1988 combined edition of the two reports, Townsend, Davidson and Whitehead note that the Black Report had been described by one observer as something like the bible: "Much quoted, occasionally read, and largely ignored when it comes to action."[17]

Underlying the judgment of the Working Group on Inequalities in Health about the measures which might be possible in the current political and economic climate [Britain in the early 1980s] runs a powerful argument, these authors say: that "a positive health strategy depends on political and economic priorities." They have some pointed comments on the distinction between the public and private sectors and collective responsibility that are worth repeating here:

The conventional wisdom is that expenditure on the welfare state, including health, is "unproductive," and that the amounts available for welfare depend on the prosperity of the private sector — which tends to be equated with the prosperity of the national economy as a whole. On these assumptions, government has no choice but to reduce welfare spending during periods of recession. Welfare spending came to be seen as something different from economic growth: at best neutral, at worst a potential "burden" on growth. Governments of all political persuasions have repeated the message: yet it is a distortion of reality.

"To see welfare merely as a potential by-product from economic growth, and as having no contribution to make to that growth," say these authors, "is at best shortsighted and at worst profoundly misguided. What requires at least as much consideration is the possibility that according to the pursuit of social objectives there may be beneficial by-products for the economy."[18]

Whether it is based on a comparison with other equally rich societies; on the demonstrated need in our own society [Britain]; or on the health benefits which accrue for lessening inequality; Townsend, Davidson and Whitehead say there is an impressive case to be made for a more generous national commitment of resources to lessening inequality. But they also observe that "These arguments, however, are not in favour today."

They note that 1979 saw the election in Britain of a Conservative government strongly committed to the values of the market-place and private enterprise. It tried to apply business management techniques to the National Health Service, for example, and it substituted efficiency for need. "Cost-benefit analysis and its associated disciplines which serve the ideology of the containment or reduction of public expenditure have come to dominate our thinking," these authors wrote in their 1988 introduction. Parts of the NHS were privatized, competing forms of external private service were subsidized, and the entire structure of the NHS was encouraged to conform with the private sector model.

Behind the Thatcher government's approach to health care was "a tenacious set of market values; a belief in the virtue of individualism — that people should have the 'freedom' to buy the best medical care they can afford, and that those who are able and willing to pay more should get more."[19] Against this, say these authors, were those of all political colours who had for four decades favoured a very strong NHS that emphasized the importance of collective responsibility and equal access to medical attention regardless of individual, financial, social or cultural constraints. These are two different versions of society. It is this difference which, more than anything else, seemed to underlie the Conservative government's denial of "inequalities in health."[20]

In *The Health Divide,* Whitehead presented evidence that confirmed serious social inequalities in health in Britain had persisted into the 1980s. Whether social position was measured by occupational class, or by assets such as house and car ownership, or by employment status, a similar picture emerged. Those at the bottom of the social scale had much higher death rates than those at the top. This applied at every stage of life, from birth through to adulthood and well into old age.[21]

And in a later book, *The International Analysis of Poverty,* published in 1993, Townsend observes that "The emerging patterns of poverty and wealth in the United States and Britain are deeply ingrained, and are being reinforced or modified all the time by policies which are dominant in those two countries. The policies are national, city-wide and international. They reflect prevailing ideologies and theories about poverty, and therefore help to explain the nature and extent of the phenomenon."[22] In this book, which was written in association with the Michael Harrington Center for Democratic Values and Social Change at City University of New York where he was Distinguished Professor of Social Science in 1992, Townsend's thesis is that "rapidly increasing unregulated access to international markets on the part of companies, combined with increasing hierarchical control of domestic labour markets and welfare conditions by states, multinational companies and international agencies, has led to the depression of the incomes of the poor, at the same time as the enlargement of the incomes of the rich."[23]

The Rowntree *Inquiry into Income and Wealth* documented the remarkable shift in Britain, where inequality of income grew at an astonishingly fast pace from the late 1970s on. It found that, internationally, the U.K. was exceptional in the pace and the extent of the increase in inequality in the 1980s; the speed with which inequality increased in the U.K. between 1977 and 1990 was faster than in any of the other major industrialized countries, with the exception of New Zealand (which had also embarked on a massive program of "marketization" of its economy and society starting in 1984); since 1979, the lowest income groups had not benefited from economic growth; since 1977, the proportion of the population with less than half the average income had more than trebled; after 1977, the gap between low wages and high wages grew; and polarization between deprived neighbourhoods and affluent neighbourhoods gradually increased during the 1980s.[24]

Wilkinson notes that this widening of income differences was accompanied by a slowing down in the rate of improvement in national mortality rates among age groups below 45 years old, and by a widening of differences in death rates between richer and poorer areas of the country. This pattern seems to have been accompanied by an almost exactly similar pattern in the results of tests of children's reading ability.[25] But he implies that these developments might be interpreted differently, depending on one's political ideology.

Some people might argue that the widening of income differentials which overtook a number of countries during the 1980s was a clear example of an exogenous change in income distribution which led to a deterioration in the social fabric of society, he says. As to the direction of causation, Wilkinson believes the evidence is ambiguous. Those who would argue that the growth in income inequality came first would point to its source in international competition and new technology which weakened the market position of people with low levels of skill and education. (This appears to be the position taken in the social outlook published by the Applied Research Branch of HRDC, referred to earlier, where it says that individuals may have fallen behind because they could not keep up with globalization and technological change).

In contrast, however, Wilkinson says, others might argue that monetarism as an economic ideology came first, and that it always had the covert aim of weakening the bargaining power of labour and cutting back the welfare state in the hope of using increased income differentials to stimulate economic growth.[26]

It is surely not coincidental that inequalities increased most rapidly in the two countries that were apparently most committed to the free-market ideology of Margaret Thatcher and had decided to transform their economies and societies to conform with the New Right agenda. In the United States, where Reagonomics was the American equivalent of Thatcherism, the Reagan-Bush years saw sharp increases in inequality. The after-tax income of the richest 1% increased by 60% during the 1980s, and polarization was exceptional. The share of after-tax "adjusted family income" going to the richest 20% of households in the U.S. rose from 39.0% to 42.1% during that time, while the share of after-tax adjusted family income going to the poorest 20% of households fell from 6.4% to 5.6%.[27]

Similar trends were evident in the U.K., where the average annual disposable income of the richest 20% of the population rose by 40% during the 1980s. Townsend says that "This is one measure of Mrs. Thatcher's collected works. It contradicts all the presuppositions of 'trickle-down' and certainly represents the biggest shift in resources from poor to rich of the 20th century."[28]

Wilkinson admits that, instead of merely market or self-interested relations between families or households, it appears that in more egalitarian societies the public sphere of life remains a more social sphere than it does elsewhere. He also cites new evidence that social cohesion is very closely related to income distribution. A number of reports on the Britain of the 1980s documented the deterioration as inequality skyrocketed. "Social cohesion is deteriorating year by year," said Will Hutton, economics editor of the *Guardian* newspaper, in his 1995 book *The State We're In.* "The combination of repression, poorly-paid work and moral sermons offered by the right as a solution is no answer to reasonable demands of decent working and living conditions," he said.[29] But social cohesion was obviously not on the policy agenda. In this respect, one cannot help but recall Margaret Thatcher's infamous dictum that "there is no such thing as a society, there are only individuals."

In Canada, Hayes and Dunn have pointed out that material inequities have been identified as having a fundamentally large and corrosive impact on health. But they also observe that the policy implications stemming from this — that by reducing material inequities within society we will improve overall health status and reduce inequities in health — would require the body politic to overcome the entrenched asymmetries of power.[30] Ruling élites are not easily persuaded to relinquish power, these authors point out, and the economic and cultural structures that maintain inequities nationally and internationally are not easily transformed.

And, writing in the British Medical Journal, a reviewer of the CIAR book *Why Are Some People Healthy and Others Not?* wonders "why, given that the importance of social and environmental determinants of health of populations has been known for so many years, has policy taken so little account of it?" His answer is that the combination of economic interests and political influences associated with the health care industry is so powerful that a predominantly biomedical system of beliefs dominates the development and practice of health policy.[31]

As Hayes and Dunn observe, "The framework provides a mandate to take action, but the evidence alone is not enough to make change."[32]

A coordinated national effort

Reviewing what progress had been made in implementing the 37 recommendations of the Black Report, Margaret Whitehead in *The Health Divide* (which came out in 1987, seven years after) found that "a distinct lack of action at national and central level" was evident. There had been no recognizable national effort to tackle inequalities in health. But major initiatives had been taken at the grassroots level by people in the health services, local government, voluntary agencies and research units around the country in response to the deeply disturbing situation documented in the Black Report. Nevertheless, Townsend, Davidson and Whitehead note that, "without a national commitment, all this activity has, understandably, been piecemeal and largely uncoordinated."

That seems to have been Canada's experience, too. A vague commitment to implementing "healthy public policies" is clearly not enough to address the serious inequalities that now show signs of increasing and that will almost certainly have a negative impact on the health of the Canadian population. At some point, if policy-makers really are committed to the WHO goal of achieving health for all — even if it can't be done by the year 2000 — they will have to deal with inequalities in health and address the fundamental issues of poverty, unemployment, inadequate housing, material deprivation and income maldistribution.

The framework for action, proposed in the 1994 ACPH report *Strategies for Population Health: Investing in the Health of Canadians,*[33] and adopted by federal and provincial health ministers at their 1994 Halifax meeting, covered all the major influences on health, including living and working conditions; physical environment; personal health practices, individual capacity and coping skills; and health services. Early childhood development was also acknowledged as a crucial influence on health which may in turn be affected by developments in each of the four main categories listed.

There are major challenges in all these areas, the report said. The different areas are also inter-related and inter-dependent. Measures to address challenges in one area could have an impact in one of the other areas. The report lists a number of challenges involving socioeconomic issues that affect population health. In listing what it believes needs to be done, the ACPH also makes some comments on how it interprets the challenges:

- **Create a thriving and sustainable economy, with meaningful work for all.** This is an important part of ensuring a healthy population. Good jobs are related to greater health, not only because they provide people with the income they need to purchase the basic necessities of life, but also because people who have meaningful work have more choices and control in their lives and that leads to better health.

  Surveys show that Canadians believe everyone should have the right to earn an adequate income. The reality is otherwise. Continuing high unemployment — particularly among young people — presents a major barrier to making improvements in population health, says the report. "In the context of globalization and the resulting restructuring of labour markets, we must find ways to create jobs which are meaningful, adequately paid and sustainable."

- **Ensure an adequate income for all Canadians.** Reduced unemployment and a higher average income for all Canadians would improve the health of many, says the report. But the ACPH also believes that "we have long had and likely will continue to have a proportion of the population living in poverty." People with inadequate incomes are particularly vulnerable to poor health. A combination of chronic unemployment, inadequate education, inadequate nutrition and poor housing all contribute to the generally poorer level of health experienced by many Aboriginal communities and by both the working and unemployed poor throughout Canada.

  In an ideal world, everyone would have meaningful work and an adequate income. But "when individual effort has failed," says the report, most Canadians believe we have a collective responsibility to ensure that basic needs are met."

- **Reduce the number of families living in poverty in Canada.**
There is an urgent need to address the problem of families living in poverty, particularly one-parent families headed by women. Children growing up in these circumstances are not able to take full advantage of educational opportunities and are much more likely to suffer poor health throughout life. Perhaps of greatest concern, says the report, is that children who grow up in poverty are unlikely to be able to provide any better conditions for their own children and grandchildren, and so the cycle of disadvantage and deprivation is passed on from one generation to the next.

Other industrialized countries have made major achievements in reducing child poverty, says the report. Canada should put a high priority on implementing successful initiatives to address this problem.

- **An equitable distribution of income.** Income inequality results in poorer health. Although average incomes and employment rates are not as high in Canada as they are in the United States, says the report, Canada's overall health status has been consistently better. Much of this can be attributed to the fact that Canada has been more successful than the United States in preventing the distribution of income in society from widening — although Canada has a less equal distribution than some other countries.

According to this report, "The sectors involved in maintaining a fair distribution of income in Canada include the federal government, provincial governments, and the private sector."

- **Encourage life-long learning.** There are large differences across Canada in literacy rates and in the levels of education achieved. According to the report, health would be improved if all jurisdictions were able to achieve levels equal to the best in the country. Greater life expectancy, an improved quality of life, and decreased illness and death from preventable diseases could all result if the quality and level of education could be improved, says the ACPH. Provincial education ministries are primarily responsible for this, says the report, but "national leadership could serve to achieve more uniform and higher levels of education across the country."

- **Foster friendship and social support networks, in families and in communities.** Support from families, friends and community members leads to better health. Initiatives to improve social support networks tend to be the responsibility of local (regional or municipal) governments, community groups, and families, the report notes. But federal and provincial policies can also encourage the development of social support networks and the participation of those at risk. For example, government policies on social housing can help to create an environment in which single parents can develop supportive relationships, says the report.

- **Foster a healthy and sustainable environment for all.** Good health requires access to good quality air, water and food, and freedom from exposure to toxins. According to the report, improving population health requires both a sustained, thriving economy and a healthy sustainable environment. The challenge is to maintain a thriving economy while preserving the integrity of the environment and the availability of resources.

- **Ensure suitable, adequate, and affordable housing.** The physical structures of our communities have an important influence on our health, says the ACPH. There is evidence that many Canadians are not able to find suitable, adequate and affordable housing. "Through housing programs and facilitating measures, governments can assist individuals, community groups, and municipalities to solve local housing issues."
- **Foster healthy child development.** Early childhood experiences influence coping skills, resistance to health problems, and overall health and well-being for the rest of one's life. The report claims that child health and development has recently been gaining considerable attention across the country. It says among the major needs identified for action are ensuring that all children and youth have access to the necessary living conditions required for optimal health and growth; fostering strong and supportive families, care-givers and communities; and providing a comprehensive and cost-effective network of policies, programs and services for all children, youth and families that stress health promotion, prevention, protection and care.

The National Forum on Health, which began a "Dialogue with Canadians" in the fall of 1995 by visiting 34 communities across Canada and holding discussion groups, entered the second and final phase of its consultation process with the release of a consultation document in November 1996. It was based on two years of research and consultation. In a telling comment, the document says that, "Despite what is known about the determinants of health, the general public continues to be mainly concerned about health care, especially when services are perceived to be threatened. As well, *governments and public administrators have not demonstrated in their decisions any appreciation of the impact of social and economic determinants and their impact on the health of individuals and communities*"[34] (emphasis added).

Which way will policy go in Canada?

It is clear that, in spite of ample evidence of the serious impact on health of social and economic factors, there is no real commitment at the level of national policy to take any action. While the 1996 ACPH *Report on the Health of Canadians* indicates that those involved in health policy at federal, provincial and territorial levels are well aware of the challenges, some of the comments in the Report seem to imply that room for action is somehow limited.

For example, does the ACPH really believe we can "find ways to create jobs which are meaningful, adequately paid and sustainable," given "the context of globalization and the resulting restructuring of labour markets"? Or does it subscribe to the view that national governments are powerless to act in the face of globalization — what Linda McQuaig has called *The Cult of Impotence*?[35]

The mantra of globalization and the perceived need for international competitiveness are increasingly invoked to justify inaction or to explain social or economic policies that have profoundly negative consequences for population health. But global competitiveness has existed since the 16th century and yet has not been allowed to serve as an acceptable rationale for laissez-faire public policies. In effect, the invocation of "globalization" increasingly masks relations of domestic power while invoking fear of economic competitors. It is the newest ideological tool to quell domestic demands for greater equity.

As for addressing the problem of poverty in Canada, the ACPH makes the statement that "we have long had, and likely will continue to have, a proportion of the population living in poverty." The comment is reminiscent of the view expressed 2,000 years ago in biblical times that "the poor will be always with us."

And on the problem of increasing income inequality in Canada, the Report says only that "The sectors involved in maintaining a fair distribution of income in Canada include the federal government, provincial governments and the private sector." No action — such as the development of a fair tax system, increases in the minimum wage, or reinvestment in social programs — is proposed. Just what is the role of the "private sector" in correcting the widening gap between rich and poor? The Report does not suggest what it might be. In fact, the "private sector" may well have been responsible for increasing income inequality in Canada, given the marked trend to non-standard work, where 40% of women's jobs and 27% of men's jobs are now temporary, part-time, contract work, self-employment or multiple jobs.[36] Many of these jobs are poorly paid, offer no job security, and have no benefits such as pensions or sick leave. How will this trend affect income distribution and ultimately create further inequalities in health?

Where is the "national leadership" that "could serve to achieve more uniform and higher levels of education across the country" which, according to the report, could result in "greater life expectancy, an improved quality of life." The abolition of the Canada Assistance Plan and its replacement with the CHST has had a harmful impact on social programs at the provincial and local level and leaves the federal government with very little leverage to play any kind of "national leadership" role.

And what has happened to government policies on social housing, which the Report says "can help to create an environment in which single parents can develop supportive relationships"? As the Alternative Budget Papers point out, Canada's social housing programs used to be the envy of the world because they effectively harnessed local communities to meet the need for decent and affordable housing.[37] Is there still any government in Canada that makes social housing a priority? The Harris government in Ontario, for example, seems to have abandoned social housing completely. Where are the "housing programs and facilitating measures" through which "governments can assist individuals, community groups, and municipalities to solve local housing issues."

What about the "comprehensive and cost-effective network of policies, programs, and services for all children, youth and families"? The long-promised national child care program has been forgotten, and there seems to be no comprehensive network of services and programs for children or youth and their families. Junior kindergarten in Ontario, for example, has been made voluntary, and municipalities and school boards, starved for cash, have found it easy to cut such programs that are vital to early childhood development.

In its *Report on the Health of Canadians,* the ACPH says that, "To maintain the health of Canadians and reduce inequalities in health status will require a coordinated effort involving all levels of government, non-government organizations, the private sector, and both formal and informal community organizations."[38] As for action on the key socioeconomic determinants of health, there is still no sign of any concerted effort to address these problems. But there is strong pressure for policies that would move us even further down the road to a market-based system where inequalities are increased, in the same way they have been in other countries that have followed this route. There will inevitably be an impact on the health of the population.

Warning signs are evident in several important areas:

Poverty

As the number of people with low incomes has increased, some commentators have claimed that the poverty numbers are exaggerated. In fact, Christopher Sarlo, in a book published by the corporate-sponsored Fraser Institute, claims that poverty, as it has traditionally been understood, has been virtually eliminated. "It is simply not a major problem in Canada," Sarlo claims.[39] In effect, the Fraser Institute and other supporters of free market ideology propose to "eliminate" poverty by redefining it.

What they suggest is an "absolute" measure of poverty to replace the generally-accepted LICOs which are a measure of relative poverty. In developing his "poverty lines" for the Fraser Institute, Sarlo allocates people the amount of money he thinks they should have for their basic needs of food, clothing and shelter — and nothing more. According to him, a single individual needs only $24 a week for food. A couple could have a healthy diet, he says, by spending just $45 a week on food. Bread, margarine and sugar would supply 55% of this couple's daily calories, according to Sarlo.

In the context of the debate about population health, as we have seen, income distribution — or the gap between rich and poor — is even more important than just being poor. Under a system of "absolute" poverty lines, policy- makers would presumably not have to worry about "poverty" unless there were increasing numbers of people without money for minimal food, clothing and shelter. The fact that more and more people were falling behind the rest of the population would be irrelevant. Yet, for the purposes of policies to improve the health of the population, such a development would be a crucial policy issue. In effect, the advocates of absolute poverty lines seem prepared to ignore the possibility of increasing inequality which is so detrimental to population health.

Sarlo admits as much in the latest edition of his book. Prevailing "poverty lines" are in fact tools for measuring inequality, he says. "This clearly reveals that, in the minds of the developers of these lines, inequality is the more important problem. They are more offended by inequality than poverty. The relative approach," he says, "rests squarely on this ideological bias and any thorough critique must challenge this premise." But Sarlo tells us that he is "not at all offended by inequality."[40]

Policy-makers concerned about population health, however, must pay attention to inequality. And they cannot make the problem of poverty go away by simply redefining it — as Sarlo has done — so that there are no poor people left.

In this context, it is perhaps relevant to note that federal, provincial and territorial social services ministers have now launched an initiative, with the assistance of Human Resources Development Canada, to develop a needs-based measure of poverty which apparently will be used to evaluate the effectiveness of the National Child Benefit. Official approval of such an absolute measure of poverty as an alternative to Statistics Canada's Low-Income Cut-Offs would appear to be an attempt to minimize the numbers of "poor" people. By emphasizing absolute rather than relative poverty, governments seem to be moving away from their commitment to address population health by trying to reduce income inequalities.

Unemployment
While many of the reports on population health referred to earlier have pointed out how the overall health of the popu-

lation is affected by high unemployment, the conventional wisdom seems to be that nothing can be done about it. Politicians talk at length about the need to "get the fundamentals right" and the rest will follow. In his 1998 budget, for example, the Finance Minister claimed that, "With the difficult stage of deficit reduction largely completed across the country, and the direct impact of public sector job cuts now largely behind us, the underlying momentum of the private sector should become more evident."[41] But he set no target for reducing unemployment. He said only that "private sector forecasters expect that the trend toward strong job creation will continue in 1998."

Economic policy in Canada has been rooted in the idea that unemployment had to be deliberately maintained at 8.5% or higher, in the interests of keeping workers economically disempowered, restraining wage increases, and maintaining ultra-low inflation.[42] This policy of official unemployment — often called the "non-accelerating inflation rate of unemployment" or NAIRU — has been promoted by the Department of Finance and other like-minded economists. The Bank of Canada's policy of zero inflation has deliberately created high unemployment and, according to Paul Krugman, a professor at the Massachusetts Institute of Technology in Boston, has cost Canadians hundreds of thousands of jobs.[43] Progressive economists have opposed the policy. The Alternative Federal Budget, for example, states that there is no "natural" rate of unemployment."[44]

Nevertheless, it would appear the Bank of Canada and the Finance Department still officially subscribe to the view that unemployment in Canada cannot fall below 8.5% without sparking off an accelerating cycle of inflation. And owners of financial wealth are demanding that the Bank clamp down on growth, reining in Canada's economy to what they consider a more "sustainable" 2.5% rate of expansion. This is consistent with their preference that unemployment be maintained in a range between 8% and 9%.[45]

Income distribution

There are several measures that might be taken to narrow the gap between rich and poor and improve income distribution, but there are no signs that governments, either federal or provincial, are planning to take any of them. Over the past couple of decades, the tax system has become less progressive through the reduction in the number of tax brackets and the introduction of the GST. Undoubtedly, as provincial costs are downloaded onto municipalities, and new assessment systems are introduced — and Ontario is a good example — local governments will almost certainly have to raise property taxes and charge user fees, both of which are regressive taxes because they bear no relation to ability to pay. Unlike virtually all other OECD countries, including the United States, Canada still does not have a wealth tax. Some people have even lobbied in favour of a single income tax rate, or flat tax.

A coalition of more than 50 national community groups, labour organizations and social policy activists, who meet each year to prepare an Alternative Federal Budget (AFB), have presented a blueprint for a system of fair taxation which could improve income distribution and ultimately contribute to improving population health. The Ontario Fair Tax Commission, which reported in December 1993 after a three-year study of the tax system, also developed proposals for improving tax fairness.

Other measures that would address the problem include the indexing of benefits such as pensions to wages rather than prices. In the long run, wages tend to rise faster than prices, so that, if social benefits are indexed to prices, people who must count on these benefits to survive fall further and further behind the rest of the population. If benefits were indexed to wages, however, the relationship between the general population and those who are surviving on various kinds of benefits would be maintained and the gap wouldn't widen any further.

Policy alternatives

Each year, the AFB attempts to address the socioeconomic issues that play such a key role in determining the health of our population. For example, the 1998 AFB emphasized income redistribution; giving relief to low- and middle-income people; reinvesting in public infrastructure; creating jobs; and other measures to reduce poverty and inequality. It was designed as an integrated program for economic and social change, while at the same time maintaining a commitment to a balanced budget.

The 1998 AFB also set a number of policy goals which would specifically address some of the socioeconomic issues that have been discussed through this report. For example, it proposed policies to reduce the official unemployment rate to 5% or lower by the end of 2001, and it set a target of reducing the poverty rate by at least six percentage points over the next four years. On this issue, the coalition recognized "the multiple causes and faces of Canadian poverty" and proposed multiple solutions to address them.[46] The coalition said the central message of hope in the AFB is that there are sensible and credible progressive alternatives to the current government's policy direction.

Policy-makers have recognized the need to address the socioeconomic basis for population health if Canada is ever to achieve its goal of health for all. Unfortunately, as noted earlier, setting out the framework for action is no guarantee that changes will be made.

Endnotes

Chapter 1

1 World Health Organization (1996) *Evaluating the Implementation of the Strategy for Health for All by the Year 2000,* Geneva.

2 Lalonde, Marc (1974) *A New Perspective on the Health of Canadians: A Working Document,* Ottawa: Health and Welfare Canada.

3 *Ibid.*

4 Epp, Jake (1986) *Achieving Health for All: A Framework for Health Promotion,* Ottawa.

5 *Ibid.* p. 6.

6 Description taken from Hamilton, Nancy and Tariq Bhatti (1996) *Population Health Promotion: An Integrated Model of Population Health and Health Promotion,* Ottawa: Health Promotion Development Division, Health Canada.

7 *Ibid.*

8 *Ibid.*

9 Hayes, Michael V. and James R. Dunn (1998) *Population Health in Canada: A Systematic Review,* CPRN Study No. H/01, Ottawa: Canadian Policy Research Networks Inc, p. 7.

10 *Ibid.* p. 48.

11 Marmor, T.R., M.L. Barer, and R.G. Evans (1994) "The Determinants of a Population's Health: What Can Be Done to Improve a Democratic Nation's Health Status?" in *Why are Some People Healthy and Others Not? The Determinants of the*

Health of Populations, edited by Robert G. Evans, Morris L. Barer and Theodore R. Marmor, New York: Aldine De Gruyter.

12 *Supra* note 9, p. 7

13 *Supra* note 9.

14 *Ibid.* p. 1.

15 Townsend, Peter, Peter Phillimore and Alastair Beattie (1988) *Health and Deprivation- Inequality and the North,* London: Croom Helm.

16 Townsend, Peter and Nick Davidson (eds.) (1982) *Inequalities in Health - The Black Report,* London: Penguin Books, p. 2.

17 Federal, Provincial and Territorial Advisory Committee on Population Health, (1994) *Strategies for Population Health: Investing in the Health of Canadians.*

18 Federal, Provincial and Territorial Advisory Committee on Population Health (1996) *Report on the Health of Canadians,* prepared for the Meeting of Ministers of Health, Toronto, September 10-11, Ottawa: Minister of Supply and Services Canada.

19 *Ibid.* p. 69.

20 *Supra* note 9, p. 39.

21 *Supra* note 9, p. 49.

22 Hayes, Foster and Foster (eds) (1994) *The Determinants of Health: A Critical Assessment,* Victoria: University of Victoria, Western Geographic Series, Vol. 29.

23 *Ibid.*

24 *Ibid.* p. 9.

25 *Supra* note 9, p. 6.

26 Wilkinson, Richard G. (1996) *Unhealthy Societies: The Afflictions of Inequality,* London: Routledge.

27 *Supra* note 6, p. 5.

28 *Supra* note 6.

29 *Supra* note 11, p. 227.

30 Marmor, T.R. (1989) "Healthy Public Policy: What Does That Mean, Who Is Responsible for It, and How Would One Pursue It?" Internal document #6A, Program in Population Health, Canadian Institute for Advanced Research, Toronto (August).

31 *Supra* note 6, p. 227.

32 *Supra* note 6, p. 225.

33 *Supra* note 16, p. 3.

34 Whitehead, Margaret (1988) *The Health Divide,* London: Penguin Books.

35 *Supra* note 16, p. 10.

36 Renaud, Marc (1994) "The Future: Hygeia Versus Panakeia?" in *Why Are Some People Healthy and Others Not?* edited by Robert G. Evans, Morris L. Barer and Theodore R. Marmor, New York: Aldine De Gruyter.

Chapter 2

1 Canadian Public Health Association (1997) *Health Impacts of Social and Economic Conditions: Implications for Public Policy,* Ottawa.

2 Health Canada Communications and Consultations Directorate (1996) *Report on the Health of Canadians,* Prepared for the Meeting of Ministers of Health, Toronto, September 10-11.

3 *Ibid.* p. 3.

4 World Health Organization (1996) *Evaluating the Implementation of the Strategy for Health for All by the Year 2000,* Geneva. p. 6.

5 *Ibid.* p. 10.

6 Lalonde, Marc (1974) *A New Perspective on the Health of Canadians: A Working Document,* Ottawa: Health and Welfare Canada.

7 *Supra* note 2.

8 Federal, Provincial and Territorial Advisory Committee on Population Health (1994) *Strategies for Population Health: Investing in the Health of Canadians,* Ottawa.

9 *Supra* note 2. p. 28.

10 *Supra* note 2, p. 22.

11 Wilkinson, Richard G. (1996) *Unhealthy Societies: The Afflictions of Inequality,* London: Routledge, p. 133.

12 *Ibid.* p. 167.

13 Poland et al. (1998) "Wealth, Equity and Health Care: A Critique of a "Population Health" Perspective on the Determinants of Health," *Social Science and Medicine.* Cited in Michael V. Hayes and James R. Dunn (1998) *Population Health in Canada: A Systematic Review,* CPRN Study No. H/01 Ottawa: Canadian Policy Research Networks Inc, p. 34.

14 *Supra* note 2 *Technical Appendix.*

15 Reid, D.D., G.Z. Brett, P.J.S. Hamilton, R.J. Jarett, H. Keen and G. Rose (1974) *Cardiorespiratory Disease and Diabetes Among Middle-Aged Male Civil Servants*, London: Lancet 1971, I, 469-73.

16 Marmot, Michael (1993) *Explaining Socioeconomic Differences in Sickness Absence: The Whitehall II Study*, Toronto: Canadian Institute for Advanced Research.

17 Marmot, Michael (1995) *In Sickness and in Wealth: the Social Causes of Illness*, Toronto: Canadian Institute for Advanced Research.

18 *Supra* note 13.

19 Evans, Robert G., Morris L. Barer and Theodore R. Marmor (eds.) (1994) *Why Are Some People Healthy and Others Not?* New York: Aldine De Gruyter, p. 93

20 *Supra* note 16, p. 9.

21 Marsh, L., A.G. Grant and C.F. Blackler (1938) *Health and Unemployment: Some Studies of their Relationships*, Montreal: McGill Social Research Series No. 7.

22 *Ibid.* pp. 215-216.

23 Hay, David I. (1993) *Does Money Buy Health? An Empirical Investigation of the Relationship Between Income and Health*, Vancouver, Social Planning and Research Council of British Columbia.

24 *Ibid.*, p. 16.

25 *Ibid.* p. 34.

26 Wilkins, R. (1995) *Mortality by Neighbourhood Income in Urban Canada, 1986-1991*, Paper presented at the Conference of the Canadian Society for Epidemiology and Biostatistics (CSEB), St. John's, Newfoundland, 16-19 August 1995.

27 Townsend, Peter and Nick Davidson (eds.) (1982) *Inequalities in Health - The Black Report*, London: Penguin Books.

28 *Supra* note 2, p. 76.

29 Statistics Canada (1994-95) *National Population Health Survey,* micro data, Ottawa: original analysis done by Tom Stephens for the *Report on the Health of Canadians.*

30 *Supra* note 1, p. 19.

31 *Ibid.*

32 *Supra* note 2, p. 50.

33 Statistics Canada (1998) *The Daily,* Ottawa: April 14, 1998.

34 *Ibid.*

35 Mustard, J. Fraser, and Frank, John (1991) *The Determinants of Health,* Toronto: Canadian Institute for Advanced Research, Publication No. 5.

36 Hertzman, C. (1994) "The Lifelong Impact of Childhood Experiences: A Population Health Perspective," *Daedalus,* Journal of the American Academy of Arts and Sciences, Fall 1994, 67-92.

37 *Supra* note 1, p. 9.

38 *Ibid.*

39 Frank, John W. (1995) *The Determinants of Health: A New Synthesis,* CIAR Program in Population Health, Working Paper No. 54, Toronto: Canadian Institute for Advanced Research.

40 *Supra* note 26.

41 Ross, David P., Katherine Scott and Mark Kelly (1996) *Child Poverty: What Are the Consequences?* Ottawa: Canadian Council on Social Development, Centre for International Statistics.

42 *Supra* note 2, p. 38.

43 National Council of Welfare (1995) *Poverty Profile 1995,* A Report by the National Council of Welfare, Ottawa, p. 1.

44 Statistics Canada, (1997) *Income Distributions by Size in Canada, 1996,* Ottawa, p. 24.

45 *Supra* note 2, p. 30.

46 *Supra* note 1, p. 16.

47 Young, T.K. et al. (1991) *The Health Effects of Housing and Community Infrastructure on Canadian Indian Reserves*, Ottawa: Department of Indian and Northern Affairs Canada.

48 Canadian Centre for Policy Alternatives (1998) *Alternative Federal Budget Papers 1998*, Ottawa: Canadian Centre for Policy Alternatives and CHO!CES: A Coalition for Social Justice, p. 153.

49 *Supra* note 33.

50 Townsend, Peter and Nick Davidson (eds.) (1982) *Inequalities in Health - The Black Report*, London: Penguin Books, p.52.

51 National Council of Welfare (1997) *Poverty Profile 1995*, A Report by the National Council of Welfare, Ottawa.

52 *Ibid.* p. 46.

53 Whitehead, Margaret (1988) *The Health Divide*, London: Penguin Books, p. 297.

54 *Op.cit.* p. 73.

55 *Supra* note 11, p. 179.

56 *Supra* note 2, p. 61.

57 *Supra* note 48, p. 153.

58 *Supra* note 1, p. 23.

59 *Ibid.*

60 *Ibid.* p. 24.

61 *Supra* note 2, p. 50.

62 Statistics Canada (1998) *Labour Force Update: An Overview of the 1997 Labour Market*, Ottawa: Winter 1998, p. 27.

63 *Ibid.* p. 29.

64 Canadian Public Health Association (1996) *The Health Impact of Unemployment*, Ottawa.

65 Canadian Centre for Policy Alternatives (1998) *The Alternative Federal Budget*, Ottawa.

66 *Supra* note 48, p. 116.

67 National Council of Welfare (1998) *Welfare Incomes 1996: A Report by the National Council of Welfare,* Ottawa: Winter 1997-98.

68 *Supra* note 4.

69 *Supra* note 64.

70 Smith, R. (1991) "Unemployment: Here We Go Again," *British Medical Journal,* Mar.16; 302(6777): 606-607. 1991; 45: 16-18.

71 Frey, J. (1982) "Unemployment and Health in the U.S.," *British Medical Journal,* April 10: 284.

72 Jin, Robert L., Chandrakant P. Shah and Tomislav J. Svoboda (1994) *The Health Impact of Unemployment: A Review and Application of Research Evidence,* Toronto: Ontario Medical Association.

73 *Ibid.* p. iii.

74 Statistics Canada (1997) *Labour Force Annual Averages 1996,* Ottawa, Table 1.

75 *Supra* note 72, p. 6.

76 *Ibid.* p. 33.

77 Statistics Canada (1995) *Women in Canada: A Statistical Report,* Third Edition, Ottawa: Ministry of Industry, p. 88.

78 *Supra* note 62, Appendix Table 6.

79 *Supra* note 72.

80 D'Arcy, C. (1986) "Unemployment and Health: Data and Implications," *Canadian Journal of Public Health,* May/June, 77: 124-131.

81 *Supra* note 62, p. 6.

82 See for example Luxton, Meg (1980) *More Than a Labour of Love: Three Generations of Women's Work in the Home,* Toronto: The Women's Press.

83 Bakker, Isabella and Diane Elson (1998) "Towards Engendering Budgets," in *Alternative Federal Budget Papers 1998,*

Ottawa: Canadian Centre for Policy Alternatives and CHO!CES: A Coalition for Social Justice. p. 309.

84 Statistics Canada (1997) *Income Distributions by Size in Canada - 1996*, Ottawa, p. 50.

85 *Supra* note 43, p. 6.

86 *Supra* note 44, Text table III.

87 Statistics Canada (1997) *A Portrait of Seniors in Canada*, Second Edition, Table 7.6, Ottawa.

88 Ross, D.P., E.R. Shillington and C. Lochhead (1994) *The Canadian Fact Book on Poverty 1994*, Ottawa: Canadian Council on Social Development.

89 *Supra* note 84, p. 22.

90 Statistics Canada (1997) *Labour Force Update: The Self-employed*, Ottawa: Autumn 1997, p. 7.

91 *Supra* note 44, p. 22.

92 *Supra* note 11, . 1.

93 *Ibid.* p. 16.

94 *Ibid.* p. 2.

95 *Ibid.* p. 78.

96 *Ibid.* p. ix.

97 Hills, John (1995) *Inquiry into Income and Wealth, Vol. 2.: A Summary of the Evidence*, York: Joseph Rowntree Foundation.

98 *Ibid.* p. 24.

99 Hutton, Will (1995) *The State We're In*, London: Vintage.

100 *Supra* note 97, p. 72.

101 *Supra* note 11, p. 98.

102 *Ibid.* p. 99.

103 *Ibid.* p. 4.

104 Brink, Satya and Allen Zeesman (1997) *Measuring Social Well-Being: An Index of Social Health for Canada*, Ottawa: Human Resources Development Canada, Applied Research Branch, Strategic Policy Research Paper R-97-9E.

105 *Ibid.* p. 9.

106 Martin, Paul (1998) *The Budget Plan 1998: Strong Economy & Secure Society*, Tabled in the House of Commons, February 24, 1998.

107 *Supra* note 11, p. 113.

108 *Ibid.* p. 8.

109 *Ibid.* p. 136.

110 *Supra* note 2, p. 71.

111 Sharpe, Andrew and Myles Zyblock (1997) *Macroeconomic Performance and Income Distribution in Canada*, Ottawa: Applied Research Branch, Strategic Policy, Human Resources Development Canada, Working Paper W-97-8E.

112 Caledon Institute (1997) *Persistent Poverty*, Caledon Statement, Ottawa: December 1997.

113 *Ibid.*

114 Statistics Canada (1997) *Income After Tax, Distributions by Size in Canada 1995*, Ottawa, p. 22.

115 *Supra* note 44, p. 20.

116 *Supra* note 2, p. 39.

117 *Supra* note 1, p. 10.

Chapter 3

1 Human Resources Development Canada (1995) *Applied Research Bulletin,* Vol. 1, Number 2, Summer 1995, Ottawa: Applied Research Branch, Human Resources Development Canada.

2 Statistics Canada (1997) *Labour Force Annual Averages 1996,* Ottawa, Table 27.

3 McCracken, Mike and Katherine Scott (1998) *Social and Economic Indicators: Underlying Assumptions, Purposes, and Values,* Ottawa: Statistics Canada Symposium on Gender Equality Indicators: Public Concerns and Public Policies, March 1998, p. 3.

4 *Ibid.* p. 4.

5 *Ibid.*

6 Canadian Council on Social Development (1996) *Measuring Well-Being: Proceedings from a Symposium on Social Indicators,* Ottawa: Final Report.

7 Oregon Progress Board (1996) *Governing for Results: Using Benchmarks to Define and Measure Progress Toward Strategic Priorities,* Salem, Oregon.

8 See http://www.econ.state.or.us/opb/OR_OPT/index.htm

9 Innes, Judith (1990) *Knowledge and Public Policy: The Search for Meaningful Indicators,* New Brunswick, NJ: Transaction Publishers.

10 *Supra* note 3, p. 4.

11 Townson, Monica (1998) *Paradigms Implicit in Social and Economic Indicators,* Presentation to the Canadian Symposium on Gender Equality Indicators: Public Concerns and Public Policies, Ottawa: Statistics Canada, March 26, 1998.

12 Martin, Paul (1998) *The Budget Plan 1998: Strong Economy & Secure Society,* Tabled in the House of Commons, February 24, 1998.

13 Federal, Provincial and Territorial Advisory Committee on Population Health (1996) *Report on the Health of Canadians,* prepared for the Meeting of Ministers of Health, Toronto, September 10-11, Ottawa: Minister of Supply and Services Canada, p. 39.

14 *Ibid.* p. 69.

15 Townsend, Peter and Nick Davidson (eds.) (1982) *Inequalities in Health - The Black Report,* London: Penguin Books, p. xi.

16 *Ibid.* p. 13.

17 *Ibid.* p. 16.

18 *Ibid.* p. 19.

19 *Ibid.* p. 27.

20 *Ibid.* p. 27.

21 Whitehead, Margaret (1988) *The Health Divide,* London: Penguin Books, p. 351.

22 Townsend, Peter (1993) *The International Analysis of Poverty,* Hemel Hempstead: Harvester Wheatsheaf, p. 18.

23 *Ibid.* p. 26.

24 Joseph Rowntree Foundation (1995) *Inquiry into Income and Wealth,* York: Joseph Rowntree Foundation.

25 Wilkinson, Richard G. (1996) *Unhealthy Societies: The Afflictions of Inequality,* London: Routledge, p. 159.

26 *Ibid.* p. 135.

27 *Supra* note 22, p. 16.

28 *Ibid.*

29 Hutton, Will (1995) *The State We're In,* London: Vintage.

30 Hayes, Michael V. and James R. Dunn (1998) *Population Health in Canada: A Systematic Review,* CPRN Study No. H/01 Ottawa: Canadian Policy Research Networks Inc., p. 58.

31 Judge, K. (1994) "Beyond Health Care: Attention Should be Directed at the Social Determinants of Ill Health," *British Medical Journal,* 309 (6967): 1454-1455. December 3, 1994. Cited in Hayes, Michael V. and James R. Dunn (1998) *Population Health in Canada: A Systematic Review,* CPRN Study No. H/01, Ottawa: Canadian Policy Research Networks Inc.

32 *Supra* note 30, p. 59.

33 Federal, Provincial and Territorial Advisory Committee on Population Health (1994) *Strategies for Population Health: Investing in the Health of Canadians,* Ottawa: Minister of Supply and Services.

34 National Forum on Health (1996) *Advancing the Dialogue on Health and Health Care: A Consultation Document,* Ottawa, p. 9.

35 McQuaig, Linda (1998) *The Cult of Impotence: Selling the Myth of Powerlessness in the Global Economy,* Toronto: Viking.

36 Townson, Monica (1997) *Non-Standard Work: The Implications for Pension Policy and Retirement Readiness,* Ottawa: Women's Bureau, Human Resources Development Canada (unpublished).

37 Canadian Centre for Policy Alternatives (1998) *Alternative Federal Budget Papers 1998,* Ottawa: Canadian Centre for Policy Alternatives and CHO!CES: A Coalition for Social Justice, p. 153.

38 *Supra* note 13, p. 76.

39 Sarlo, Christopher A. (1996) *Poverty in Canada,* 2nd edition, Vancouver: The Fraser Institute, p. 2.

40 *Ibid.* p. 3.

41 *Supra* note 12, p. 33.

42 *Supra* note 37, p. 18.

43 *Supra* note 35, p. 105.

44 *Supra* note 37, p. 19.

45 *Supra* note 37, p. 58

Health and Wealth

SELECTED BIBLIOGRAPHY

Bakker, Isabella and Diane Elson (1998) "Towards Engendering Budgets," in *Alternative Federal Budget Papers 1998,* Ottawa: Canadian Centre for Policy Alternatives and CHO!CES: A Coalition for Social Justice.

Brink, Satya and Allen Zeesman (1997) *Measuring Social Well-Being: An Index of Social Health for Canada,* Ottawa: Human Resources Development Canada, Applied Research Branch, Strategic Policy Research Paper R-97-9E.

Caledon Institute (1997) *Persistent Poverty,* Ottawa: December 1997.

Canadian Centre for Policy Alternatives (1998) *Alternative Federal Budget Papers 1998,* Ottawa: Canadian Centre for Policy Alternatives and CHO!CES: A Coalition for Social Justice.

Canadian Centre for Policy Alternatives (1998) *The 1998 Alternative Federal Budget,* Ottawa.

Canadian Council on Social Development (1996) *Measuring Well-Being: Proceedings form a Symposium on Social Indicators,* Ottawa: Final Report.

Canadian Public Health Association (1996) *The Health Impact of Unemployment,* Ottawa.

Canadian Public Health Association (1997) *Health Impacts of Social and Economic Conditions: Implications for Public Policy,* Ottawa.

D'Arcy, C. (1986) "Unemployment and Health: Data and Implications," *Canadian Journal of Public Health,* May/June.

Epp, Jake (1986) *Achieving Health for All: A Framework for Health Promotion,* Ottawa.

Evans, Robert G., Morris L. Barer and Theodore R. Marmor (eds.) (1994) *Why Are Some People Healthy and Others Not?* New York: Aldine De Gruyter.

Federal, Provincial and Territorial Advisory Committee on Population Health (1994) *Strategies for Population Health: Investing in the Health of Canadians.*

Federal, Provincial and Territorial Advisory Committee on Population Health (1996) *Report on the Health of Canadians,* prepared for the Meeting of Ministers of Health, Toronto, September 10-11, Ottawa: Minister of Supply and Services Canada.

Frank, John W. (1995) *The Determinants of Health: A New Synthesis,* CIAR Program in Population Health, Working Paper No. 54, Toronto: Canadian Institute for Advanced Research.

Frey, J. (1982) "Unemployment and Health in the U.S." *British Medical Journal,* April 10: 284.

Hamilton, Nancy and Tariq Bhatti (1996) *Population Health Promotion: An Integrated Model of Population Health and Health Promotion,* Ottawa: Health Promotion Development Division, Health Canada.

Hay, David I. (1993) *Does Money Buy Health? An Empirical Investigation of the Relationship Between Income and Health,* Vancouver, Social Planning and Research Council of British Columbia.

Hayes, Foster and Foster (eds) (1994) *The Determinants of Health: A Critical Assessment,* Victoria: University of Victoria Western Geographic Series, Vol. 29.

Hayes, Michael V. and James R. Dunn (1998) *Population Health in Canada: A Systematic Review,* CPRN Study No. H/01, Ottawa: Canadian Policy Research Networks Inc.

Health Canada Communications and Consultations Directorate (1996) *Report on the Health of Canadians,* Ottawa: Prepared for the Meeting of Ministers of Health, Toronto, September 10-11.

Hertzman, C. (1994) "The Lifelong Impact of Childhood Experiences: A Population Health Perspective," *Daedalus,* Journal of the American Academy of Arts and Sciences, Fall 1994.

Hills, John (1995) *Inquiry into Income and Wealth, Vol. 2.: A Summary of the Evidence,* York: Joseph Rowntree Foundation.

Human Resources Development Canada (1995) *Applied Research Bulletin,* Vol. 1, Number 2, Summer 1995, Ottawa: Applied Research Branch, Human Resources Development Canada.

Hutton, Will (1995) *The State We're In,* London: Vintage.

Innes, Judith (1990) *Knowledge and Public Policy: The Search for Meaningful Indicators,* New Brunswick, N.J.: Transaction Publishers.

Jin, Robert L., Chandrakant P. Shah and Tomislav J. Svoboda (1994) *The Health Impact of Unemployment: A Review and Application of Research Evidence,* Toronto: Ontario Medical Association.

Joseph Rowntree Foundation (1995) *Inquiry into Income and Wealth,* York: Joseph Rowntree Foundation.

Judge, K. (1994) "Beyond Health Care: Attention Should be Directed at the Social Determinants of Ill Health," *British Medical Journal* 309 (6967): 1454-1455, December 3, 1994. Cited in Hayes, Michael V. and James R. Dunn (1998) *Population Health in Canada: A Systematic Review,* CPRN Study No. H/01, Ottawa: Canadian Policy Research Networks Inc.

Lalonde, Marc (1974) *A New Perspective on the Health of Canadians: A Working Document,* Ottawa: Health and Welfare Canada.

Luxton, Meg (1980) *More Than a Labour of Love: Three Generations of Women's Work in the Home,* Toronto: The Women's Press.

Marmor, T.R. (1989) "Healthy Public Policy: What Does That Mean, Who Is Responsible for It, and How Would One Pursue It?" Internal document #6A, Program in Population Health, Canadian Institute for Advanced Research, Toronto (August).

Marmor, T.R., M.L. Barer and R.G. Evans (1994) "The Determinants of a Population's Health: What Can Be Done to Improve a Democratic Nation's Health Status?" in *Why are Some People Healthy and Others Not? The Determinants of the Health of Populations,* edited by Robert G. Evans, Morris L. Barer and Theodore R. Marmor, New York: Aldine De Gruyter.

Marmot, Michael (1993) *Explaining Socioeconomic Differences in Sickness Absence: The Whitehall II Study,* Toronto: Canadian Institute for Advanced Research.

Marmot, Michael (1995) *In Sickness and in Wealth: the Social Causes of Illness,* Toronto: Canadian Institute for Advanced Research.

Marsh, L., A.G. Grant and C.F. Blackler (1938) *Health and Unemployment: Some Studies of Their Relationships,* Montreal: McGill Social Research Series No. 7.

Martin, Paul (1998) *The Budget Plan 1998: Strong Economy & Secure Society,* Tabled in the House of Commons, February 24, 1998.

McCracken, Mike and Katherine Scott (1998) *Social and Economic Indicators: Underlying Assumptions, Purposes, and Values,* Ottawa: Statistics Canada Symposium on Gender Equality Indicators: Public Concerns and Public Policies, March 1998.

McQuaig, Linda (1998) *The Cult of Impotence: Selling the Myth of Powerlessness in the Global Economy,* Toronto: Viking.

Mustard, J. Fraser and John Frank (1991) *The Determinants of Health,* Toronto: Canadian Institute for Advanced Research, Publication No. 5.

National Council of Welfare (1997) *Poverty Profile 1995,* A Report by the National Council of Welfare, Ottawa.

National Council of Welfare (1998) *Welfare Incomes 1996: A Report by the National Council of Welfare,* Ottawa: Winter 1997-98.

National Forum on Health (1996) *Advancing the Dialogue on Health and Health Care: A Consultation Document,* Ottawa.

Oregon Progress Board (1996) *Governing for Results: Using Benchmarks to Define and Measure Progress Toward Strategic Priorities,* Salem, Oregon.

Poland, et al. (1998) "Wealth, Equity and Health Care: A Critique of a "Population Health" Perspective on the Determinants of Health," *Social Science and Medicine.* Cited in Hayes, Michael V. and James R. Dunn (1998) *Population Health in Canada: A Systematic Review,* CPRN Study No. H/01, Ottawa: Canadian Policy Research Networks Inc.

Reid, D.D., G.Z. Brett, P.J.S. Hamilton, R.J. Jarett, H. Keen and G. Rose (1974) *Cardiorespiratory Disease and Diabetes Among Middle-Aged Male Civil Servants,* London: Lancet 1971, I, 469-73.

Renaud, Marc (1994) "The Future: Hygeia Versus Panakeia?" in *Why Are Some People Healthy and Others Not?* Robert G. Evans, Morris L. Barer and Theodore R. Marmor (eds.) New York: Aldine De Gruyter.

Ross, D.P., E.R. Shillington and C. Lochhead (1994) *The Canadian Fact Book on Poverty, 1994,* Ottawa: Canadian Council on Social Development.

Ross, David P., Katherine Scott and Mark Kelly (1996) *Child Poverty: What Are the Consequences?* Ottawa: Canadian Council on Social Development, Centre for International Statistics.

Sarlo, Christopher A. (1996) *Poverty in Canada,* Second Edition, Vancouver: The Fraser Institute.

Sharpe, Andrew and Myles Zyblock (1997) *Macroeconomic Performance and Income Distribution in Canada,* Ottawa: Applied Research Branch, Strategic Policy, Human Resources Development Canada, Working Paper W-97-8E.

Smith, R. (1991) "Unemployment: Here We Go Again," *British Medical Journal,* Mar.16; 302(6777): 606-607. 1991; 45: 16-18.

Statistics Canada (1994-95) *National Population Health Survey,* micro data, Ottawa: original analysis done by Tom Stephens for the *Report on the Health of Canadians.*

Statistics Canada (1995) *Women in Canada: A Statistical Report,* Third Edition, Ottawa: Ministry of Industry.

Statistics Canada (1997) *A Portrait of Seniors in Canada,* Second Edition, Ottawa.

Statistics Canada (1997) *Income After Tax, Distributions by Size in Canada, 1995,* Ottawa.

Statistics Canada (1997) *Income Distributions by Size in Canada, 1996,* Ottawa.

Statistics Canada (1997) *Labour Force Annual Averages, 1996,* Ottawa.

Statistics Canada (1997) *Labour Force Update: The Self-employed,* Ottawa: Autumn 1997.

Statistics Canada (1998) *Labour Force Update: An Overview of the 1997 Labour Market,* Ottawa: Winter 1998.

Statistics Canada (1998) *The Daily,* Ottawa: April 14, 1998.

Townsend, Peter and Nick Davidson (eds.) (1982) *Inequalities in Health — The Black Report,* London: Penguin Books.

Townsend, Peter, Peter Phillimore and Alastair Beattie (1988) *Health and Deprivation — Inequality and the North,* London: Croom Helm.

Townsend, Peter (1993) *The International Analysis of Poverty,* Hemel Hempstead: Harvester Wheatsheaf.

Townson, Monica (1997) *Non-Standard Work: The Implications for Pension Policy and Retirement Readiness,* Ottawa: Women's Bureau, Human Resources Development Canada (unpublished).

Townson, Monica (1998) *Paradigms Implicit in Social and Economic Indicators,* Presentation to the Canadian Symposium on Gender Equality Indicators: Public Concerns and Public Policies, Ottawa: Statistics Canada, March 26, 1998.

Whitehead, Margaret (1988) *The Health Divide,* London: Penguin Books.

Wilkins, R. (1995) *Mortality by Neighbourhood Income in Urban Canada, 1986-1991*, Paper presented at the Conference of the Canadian Society for Epidemiology and Biostatistics (CSEB), St. John's, Newfoundland, 16-19 August 1995.

Wilkinson, Richard G. (1996) *Unhealthy Societies: the Afflictions of Inequality*, London: Routledge.

World Health Organization (1996) *Evaluating the Implementation of the Strategy for Health for All by the Year 2000*, Geneva.

Young, T.K. et al. (1991) *The Health Effects of Housing and Community Infrastructure on Canadian Indian Reserves*, Ottawa: Department of Indian and Northern Affairs Canada.